Rome's Civil War 49–45 BC

Caesarian Legionary

VERSUS

Pompeian Legionary

COMBAT

William Horsted

Illustrated by Giuseppe Rava

OSPREY PUBLISHING
Bloomsbury Publishing Plc
Kemp House, Chawley Park, Cumnor Hill, Oxford OX2 9PH, UK
Bloomsbury Publishing Ireland Limited,
29 Earlsfort Terrace, Dublin 2, Ireland
1385 Broadway, 5th Floor, New York, NY 10018, USA
E-mail: info@ospreypublishing.com
www.ospreypublishing.com

OSPREY is a trademark of Osprey Publishing Ltd

First published in Great Britain in 2025

A catalogue record for this book is available from the British Library.

ISBN: PB 9781472867049; eBook 9781472867025;
ePDF 9781472867131; XML 9781472867032

25 26 27 28 29   10 9 8 7 6 5 4 3 2 1

Maps by bounford.com
Index by Rob Munro
Typeset by PDQ Digital Media Solutions, Bungay, UK
Printed by Repro India Ltd.

To find out more about our authors and books visit
www.ospreypublishing.com. Here you will find extracts, author
interviews, details of forthcoming events and the option to sign up for
our newsletter.

For product safety related questions contact
productsafety@bloomsbury.com

CONTENTS

Introduction

One night in early January 49 BC, a column of Roman soldiers waited on a country road in the north of Italy. Up ahead, their commander, Gaius Julius Caesar (100–44 BC), stood alone, next to a small wooden bridge. The soldiers whispered to each other in the darkness. Why had Caesar halted? What were they doing here?

Bust of Gaius Julius Caesar in the Vatican Museum in Vatican City, Italy. According to Suetonius, Caesar was skilled in the use of Roman weapons and a talented rider. He often rode at the head of his army and could endure long journeys. He was also a strong swimmer (*Iul.* 57). Though healthy for much of his life, he began to suffer from epilepsy in his final years. (Universal History Archive/Getty Images)

Caesar had stopped at the Rubicon River, which formed the boundary between Gallia Cisalpina, one of Caesar's allotted 'provinces' (from the Latin *provincia*, or 'task'), and Italy. Within his province, Caesar possessed the power of *imperium*, the right to command citizens and soldiers in the Roman Army. He had been appointed to an extraordinary ten-year command, and with his army of 12 legions of loyal and experienced soldiers, had conquered the whole of Gaul (roughly modern-day France and Belgium), crossed the Rhine River and made two expeditions to Britain. As his period of command was coming to an end, Caesar had wanted to return to Rome; but, if he left his province, he would have had to surrender his *imperium* and give up his army. He feared that his political enemies in the senate (*senatus*; Rome's ruling council) would attempt to prosecute him for alleged crimes if he entered the city as a private citizen. Caesar had tried to stand for election to become consul (the consuls were the senior magistrates (elected officials) in Rome; two were elected every year), the highest office in the Roman Republic, *in absentia*. If successful, he could have returned to Rome in safety. Caesar's enemies, however, remembered his last time as consul, in 59 BC, with horror. They feared for the stability of the Republic if he entered office again and were terrified of his veteran army. They did everything they could to force Caesar to relinquish his command.

Caesar had been prepared to compromise. He had offered to give up all but one of his 12 legions and retain only the province of Illyricum (modern-day Croatia). He was even willing to surrender command of his whole army, if Rome's other most powerful military leader, Pompey 'the Great' (Gnaeus

Pompeius Magnus, 106–48 BC), would do the same; but Caesar's enemies, who had turned to Pompey and begged him to protect the Republic, were implacable and pressed the senate to declare Caesar a public enemy. Pompey's legions were in Hispania, however; the only soldiers currently in Italy were two legions sent by Caesar for a planned campaign against the powerful Parthian (Arsacid) Empire, centred on the Iranian plateau, which had inflicted a catastrophic defeat on a Roman army at the battle of Carrhae in 53 BC. Unsurprisingly, Pompey doubted the two legions' allegiance, and immediately began to recruit fresh troops. Rome was gripped by panic, as reports spread that Caesar was approaching Italy at the head of his whole army. The senate passed 'the ultimate decree', declaring that the consuls and other Roman magistrates with *imperium* should take all necessary steps to ensure the Republic came to no harm.

Caesar had left most of his army on the other side of the Alps. He had arrived at Ravenna in the south of Gallia Cisalpina a few days before, with only the infantry of *legio XIII* (about 5,000 men) and about 300 cavalry. The rest must have been given instructions to follow. At Ravenna, Caesar had tried to disguise his intentions by spending the day in public watching gladiatorial combats. After a visit to the baths in the afternoon, he had dined with several guests in the evening and slipped away after dinner.

At the Rubicon, Caesar turned and beckoned to his officers, who were also waiting nearby. The soldiers watched as he consulted the officers in turn. One of those officers was Gaius Asinius Pollio, who recorded the conversation in his history of the civil wars. Sadly, Pollio's books have not survived, but they were used as source material by other ancient writers, including the Greek historian Appian of Alexandria, who wrote his own history of the civil wars, and the biographers Plutarch and Suetonius.

Caesar reflected on the consequences of crossing the Rubicon. He could still turn back, or he could leave his army behind and face his fate in Rome alone. If he continued into Italy with his troops, however, everything from then on would be decided by arms (Suetonius, *Iul.* 31). Caesar was suddenly resolute. He declared, 'let the die be cast', and crossed the bridge (Appian, *BCiv.* 2.35). Earlier in the day, he had sent a small force of junior officers ahead in civilian clothes to capture Ariminum (modern-day Rimini, Italy), the nearest town in Italy (Plutarch, *Vit. Caes.* 32). Just before dawn, Caesar and the rest of his men marched through the open gates of the town.

In Ariminum, Caesar was joined by three of his supporters from the senate, Gaius Scribonius Curio, Quintus Cassius Longinus and Mark Antony (Marcus Antonius). These men were tribunes of the plebs (*tribuni plebis*), magistrates in Rome tasked with safeguarding the rights of the common people against the aristocracy. Because of their support for Caesar, the three were forced to flee Rome hidden in a cart, disguised as slaves. This provided Caesar with an excellent propaganda opportunity. He gathered his troops and showed them the tribunes of the plebs, still dressed as slaves. The soldiers close enough (many were too far away to hear) listened as Caesar explained that despite all their victories on behalf of the Republic, and all they had endured on campaign in Gaul, the senate were now treating them as enemies; and when these three important men had tried to intervene on their behalf, they were forced to suffer the humiliation of being driven from Rome wearing

A bust of Pompey 'the Great' (Gnaeus Pompeius Magnus, 106–48 BC) in the Museo della Civiltà Romana in Rome, Italy. In the mid-1st century BC, Pompey was Rome's most successful general. When still a young man he had raised his own legion in support of Lucius Cornelius Sulla in 83 BC. He spent several years in Hispania fighting the Roman rebel commander Quintus Sertorius, and in 67 BC defeated pirates in the Mediterranean. He confronted Mithridates VI Eupator, the king of Pontus (r. 120–63 BC), on the southern shores of the Black Sea in modern-day Turkey. After Mithridates was killed by his son Pharnaces II (r. 63–47 BC), Pompey reorganized a huge swathe of territory of the former Seleucid kingdom in Rome's favour, doubling the revenue from Rome's overseas possessions (Tatum 2010: 197). In 59 BC he entered an informal political alliance with Marcus Licinius Crassus and Caesar – the 'First Triumvirate' – and the three men established effective control over the Republic. Caesar left for Gaul in 58 BC, and in 53 BC Crassus was killed fighting the Parthians. Tasked with overseeing Rome's grain supply, as well as the command of the two Spanish provinces, Pompey remained near Rome, and managed Hispania through his legates. (PHAS/Universal Images Group via Getty Images)

When Julius Caesar crossed the Rubicon River in early January 49 BC and began the civil war, the city of Rome sat at the centre of a growing empire. Over the previous three centuries, successive Roman commanders had conquered most of the Mediterranean basin, much of the Iberian Peninsula and the western parts of Asia Minor. The empire was divided into 'provinces' (from the Latin *provincia* or 'task'). Each province was overseen by a Roman official known as a *pro magistratu*, or governor, who was appointed by Rome's ruling council, the senate. The Roman legions were divided among the provinces, where they were placed under the command of the governors. Some governors, such as Julius Caesar in Gaul, and Pompey in Syria and Asia Minor, used the legions under their command to expand Rome's empire, bringing in enormous wealth.

Those areas not under direct Roman control were ruled by monarchies, whose power was maintained at least in part with support from the Roman senate. Mauretania was divided into two: the western kingdom of Bogus (aka Bogud; r. 49–38 BC), and the eastern kingdom of his brother Bocchus II (r. 49–33 BC). Both kings supported Caesar in the civil war. Juba I, the king of Numidia (r. 60–46 BC), was an ally of Pompey, and joined forces with Pompey's generals after the latter's death in 48 BC. Egypt had been ruled by the Ptolemaic dynasty since 305 BC, when Ptolemy I Soter (r. 305–282 BC), a leading commander under Alexander III of Macedon (aka Alexander the Great,

r. 336–323 BC), had declared himself pharaoh. His descendant, Ptolemy XII Auletes (r. *c.*80–58 BC and 55–51 BC), who had been deposed and returned to the throne of Egypt with the help of Pompey, left the kingdom jointly to his son Ptolemy XIII Theos Philopator (r. 51–47 BC) and his daughter Cleopatra VII (r. 51–30 BC). When Pompey fled to Egypt after the battle of Pharsalus in the autumn of 48 BC, the Egyptian siblings were engaged in a civil war of their own. Several eastern monarchs were also indebted to Pompey and were willing allies during the civil war.

Caesar had been governor of the provinces of Illyricum and Gallia Cisalpina since 58 BC and had been granted Gallia Transalpina soon after. In the following nine years he fought his way across the region known to the Romans as Gaul (roughly modern-day France and Belgium) and brought most of the area under Roman control. During his campaign, he expanded his army from four legions to a significant force of 12 legions. In 50 BC, he transferred two of these legions to Italy in preparation for a campaign in the East. Though Pompey remained in Italy, he commanded six legions in Spain, and there were two legions stationed in the province of Syria, which had just been granted to Pompey's fellow senator Scipio (Quintus Caecilius Metellus Pius Scipio). Though at the outbreak of civil war Pompey commanded the smaller army, he boasted that he had only to stamp his foot on the ground to fill Italy with soldiers.

slaves' tunics (Appian, *BCiv.* 2.33; Plutarch, *Vit. Caes.* 31). Caesar begged his men to defend his reputation and position. He tore at his clothes and cried (Suetonius, *Iul.* 33). He had to be sure that they would support him in a war against other Roman soldiers, and the Roman state. Caesar doubled his soldiers' pay (Suetonius, *Iul.* 26; Keppie 1984: 103) and may have promised them grants of land at the end of their service. The soldiers of *legio XIII* roared in support of their commander and swore to avenge the wrongs done to him and to the tribunes of the plebs (Caesar, *BCiv.* 1.7). Civil war had begun.

Though Pompey was the obvious choice to stop Caesar, he did not have sole authority. The two consuls were still in command of the Republic, and other senators were allotted provinces: Quintus Caecilius Metellus Pius Scipio Nasica took control of Syria, and Domitius Ahenobarbus was granted Caesar's Gallic provinces (Caesar, *BCiv.* 1.6). As Caesar marched south, Domitius occupied the town of Corfinium (modern-day Corfino), east of Rome, with a hastily recruited force of around 20 cohorts. Promising the recruits grants of 25 acres of land each, and more for re-enlisted veterans and centurions, Domitius oversaw the construction of artillery pieces and other defences (Caesar, *BCiv.* 1.17). Arriving on 17 February, Caesar's men immediately constructed siegeworks. Domitius' soldiers decided to surrender. They apprehended Domitius and four other senators and presented them to Caesar, who set them all free. Caesar made Domitius' soldiers swear a new oath of allegiance to himself and incorporated them into his army (Caesar, *BCiv.* 1.19–23).

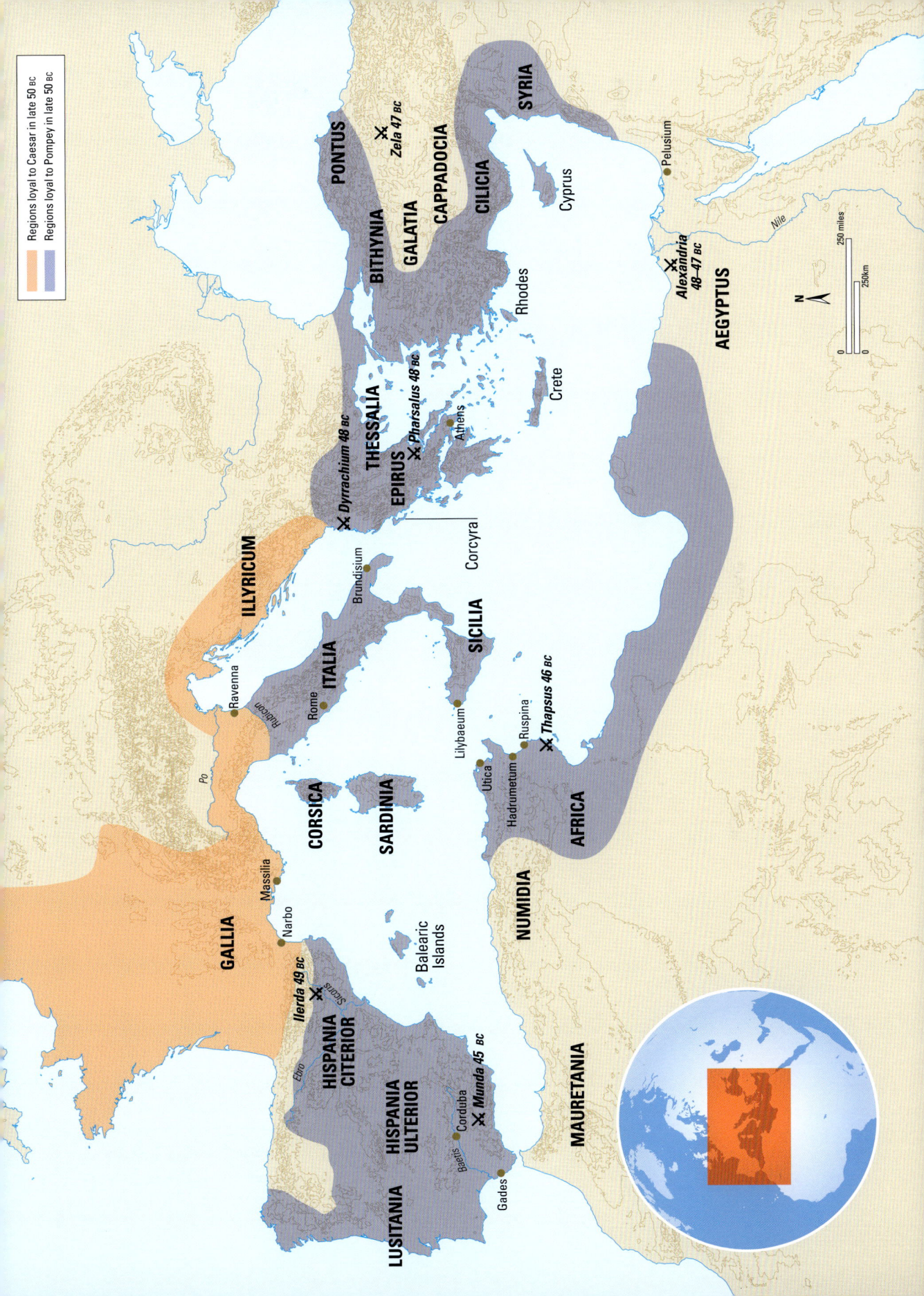

Regions loyal to Caesar in late 50 BC
Regions loyal to Pompey in late 50 BC

PONTUS
Zela 47 BC ✕
CAPPADOCIA
SYRIA
Pelusium
Nile
BITHYNIA
GALATIA
CILICIA
Cyprus
Rhodes
N
250 miles
250km
0
AEGYPTUS
Alexandria 48–47 BC ✕
THESSALIA
Dyrrachium 48 BC ✕
Pharsalus 48 BC ✕
EPIRUS
Athens
Crete
ILLYRICUM
Brundisium
Corcyra
Ravenna
ITALIA
SICILIA
Rubicon
Rome
Po
Thapsus 46 BC ✕
Ruspina
Lilybaeum
CORSICA
Utica
Hadrumetum
AFRICA
SARDINIA
Massilia
NUMIDIA
Narbo
GALLIA
Balearic Islands
Ilerda 49 BC ✕
Sicoris
HISPANIA CITERIOR
MAURETANIA
Munda 45 BC ✕
HISPANIA ULTERIOR
Corduba
Baetis
Gades
LUSITANIA

The Opposing Sides

In most respects, the armies of the two sides in the Roman civil war of 49–44 BC were indistinguishable. As many as 20 legions (more than 90,000 men) were already serving before the war began, and had been recruited, trained, organized and equipped in essentially the same way (Goldsworthy 2023: 30). During the conflict, many thousands more troops were raised from all over Roman territory, and from Rome's allies.

By the middle of the 1st century BC, many of the characteristics of the army of the Roman emperors had developed. Several legions raised by Caesar would form the basis of the army of his heir Gaius Octavius (commonly known as Octavian and later Augustus, the first Roman emperor; r. 27 BC–AD 14) in his struggle for sole control of the Roman Empire, and ultimately the core of the imperial army. Legionaries began serving longer, many for much of their adult lives, and in practice became 'professional' soldiers. Some members of the Roman elite started to focus on a military career, rather than regarding military service as strictly a necessary step towards political advancement. For example, officers such as Titus Atius Labienus, Caesar's most trusted legate (*legatus*; deputy commander), during his conquest of Gaul (and the only senior officer to desert him for Pompey) and Marcus Petreius, Pompey's legate in Hispania who commanded Roman troops with distinction for over 40 years, became expert military commanders.

Dated to 42–40 BC, this coin bears a depiction of Pompey the Great on the obverse and Anapius and Amphinomus rescuing their parents from an eruption of Mount Etna on the reverse. (Heritage Art/ Heritage Images via Getty Images)

RECRUITMENT AND MOTIVATION

Despite the changes apparent in the Roman Army in the mid-1st century BC, it retained the structure of a citizen militia. Recruitment into the legions was by means of a *dilectus* or 'choosing' from a list of eligible citizens known as the *census*. Only Roman citizens could join the legions, and it was a legal duty for all men between the ages of 17 and 46 to make themselves available for military service. Up until the end of the 2nd century BC, there had been a minimum property qualification (most legionaries were small independent farmers). This was to ensure legionaries could afford their own equipment but also because soldiers would not be financially dependent on the Roman state, or more importantly their commander. Citizens with property were able to vote in elections and were therefore actively involved in the Republic (*res publica*, literally 'the public thing'), and soldiers who owned a piece of Roman territory, however small, would be expected to fight the hardest to defend it.

Most legionaries were volunteers, though, if necessary, citizens were chosen by lot from the *census* rolls and conscripted. Until the end of the 2nd century BC, soldiers' equipment and deployment within the legion depended on their age and wealth. The poorest joined the *velites*, or unarmoured light infantry, who skirmished in front of the legions with light javelins. The youngest soldiers with sufficient property formed the *hastati*, in the first rank of the legion, and those in the prime of adulthood made up the *principes* in the second rank. The *triarii*, or 'third liners', were older veteran soldiers. The three types of heavy infantry were equipped differently. *Hastati* and *principes* carried *scuta* (large oval shields), two *pila* (heavy javelins) and *gladii* (short stabbing swords), while the *triarii* carried a *scutum* and a *hasta* (thrusting spear) in place of javelins. The very wealthiest citizens formed the cavalry. By the beginning of the 1st century BC, however, these distinctions had disappeared.

At the outbreak of Caesar's civil war, legionary recruits could expect to serve for a minimum of six years and normally up to 16 years, though many chose, or were forced, to serve for much longer. One veteran centurion in Caesar's *legio XIIII* boasted that he been fighting for 36 years when the ship in

Relief carving of a cavalry engagement on a monument to the Julii family in the Roman city of Glanum (modern-day Saint-Rémy-de-Provence, France). Though the details of armour and equipment worn by the soldiers in this artistic depiction of fighting during the civil wars of the 1st century BC may not be wholly realistic, the dramatic scene does convey the intensity of close-quarters fighting. (Albert Ceolan/ De Agostini Picture Library via Getty Images)

COMBAT Legionary, *legio X*

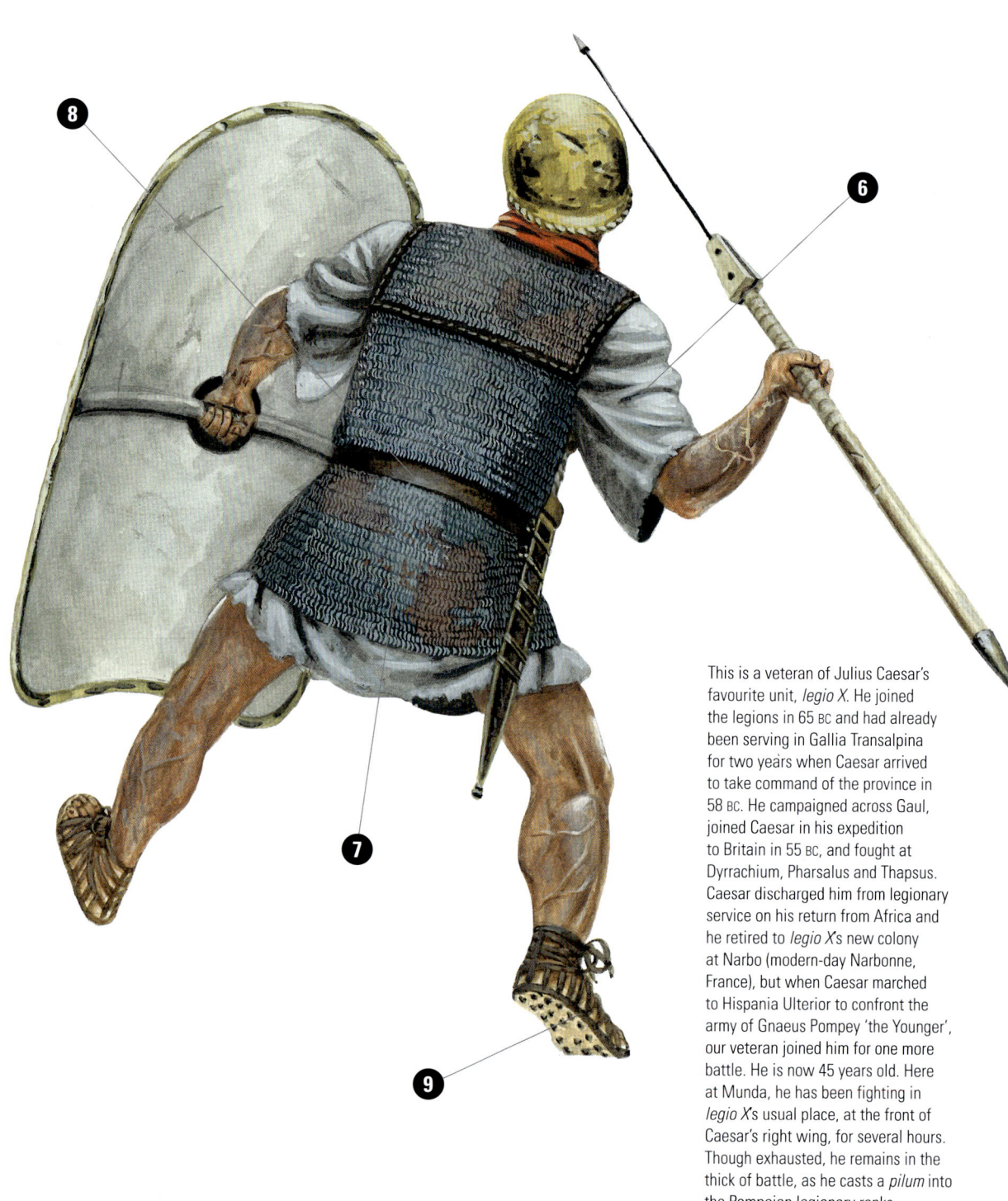

This is a veteran of Julius Caesar's favourite unit, *legio X*. He joined the legions in 65 BC and had already been serving in Gallia Transalpina for two years when Caesar arrived to take command of the province in 58 BC. He campaigned across Gaul, joined Caesar in his expedition to Britain in 55 BC, and fought at Dyrrachium, Pharsalus and Thapsus. Caesar discharged him from legionary service on his return from Africa and he retired to *legio X*'s new colony at Narbo (modern-day Narbonne, France), but when Caesar marched to Hispania Ulterior to confront the army of Gnaeus Pompey 'the Younger', our veteran joined him for one more battle. He is now 45 years old. Here at Munda, he has been fighting in *legio X*'s usual place, at the front of Caesar's right wing, for several hours. Though exhausted, he remains in the thick of battle, as he casts a *pilum* into the Pompeian legionary ranks.

Weapons, dress and equipment

This legionary has wrapped the shaft of his heavy javelin (*pilum*; **1**) with leather to make it more comfortable to carry on long marches, and to give his sweaty hands a better grip in the excitement of battle. The long, iron head is designed to punch through an enemy shield and reach the man behind and will hopefully bend on impact so it cannot be thrown back. When he has released his *pilum*, he will draw his short, sharply pointed sword (*gladius*; **2**) from its scabbard on his right hip, charge at the enemy ranks with a furious shout, and smash into the first opponent with his large, curved shield (*scutum*; **3**), large enough to protect his body from shoulder to knee. He uses the iron-covered boss (*umbo*; **4**) to punch his enemy, or he can lean his shoulder against the back of the shield and shove him aside. To protect his hand from the force of enemy blows, the inside of the boss is covered in soft wool or horsehair, and he can catch sword cuts with the reinforced rim.

His simple copper-alloy helmet (*galea*; **5**) has only a slight neck guard and no cheek pieces, so he can move his head without restriction, and see and hear everything that is going on around him. Like his ragged woollen tunic (*tunica*; **6**), his mail armour (*lorica hamata*; **7**) bears the scars of years of campaigning and has been repaired in several places; made from small iron rings welded or riveted together, it is very flexible, and provides excellent protection to his torso, abdomen and groin. Some of its weight (around 9kg) is taken up by his thick leather belt (*balteus*; **8**), and he has tucked a woollen scarf around his neck to prevent the armour chafing. His hobnailed sandals (*caligae*; **9**) provide much-needed traction on the blood-soaked ground.

which he was travelling was captured off the coast of the Roman province of Africa in 46 BC (*BAfr.* 45). In earlier centuries, when this system was devised, legionaries would be recruited in the spring for a summer of campaigning in Italy and would hope to return to their farms in time for harvest in the autumn (Keppie 1984: 33–34, 76–78). Since the war with Hannibal in the late 3rd century BC, however, most of the Roman Army's activities had been overseas, in Hispania, northern Africa and the Greek east. Legionaries were therefore away from home, and their farms, for years at a time. Recruitment became increasingly difficult, particularly for arduous conflicts, like those fought throughout the 2nd century BC in Hispania against the Celtiberians, where legions could be posted for several years, fighting was continuous, conditions harsh and the prospects of bringing home booty very poor. By contrast, recruitment for wars in the Greek east attracted more than enough volunteers. Here legionaries could expect a quick victory after a major battle, and the hope of a small share in the spoils and the profit from the sale of thousands of captured troops into slavery was a powerful draw (Sage 2018: 240).

In 112 BC, war broke out in northern Africa. Jugurtha, a former ally of Rome, had seized power from his cousins and taken sole control of Numidia (modern-day Algeria and parts of Tunisia and Libya). In the ensuing struggles his troops murdered several Italian merchants, and the Roman senate was forced to intervene. Jugurtha easily defeated the first Roman army sent against him, and subsequent generals had no more success. In 109 BC, the consul Quintus Caecilius Metellus, a member of a famous senatorial family, raised extra troops and set about improving the effectiveness of the Roman Army through rigorous training. He was assisted by a staff of skilled and experienced officers, including Gaius Marius, a senator from relatively humble origins. Marius was enormously ambitious. He exploited the Roman people's impatience with Metellus' strategy and succeeded in becoming consul in 107 BC, partly by portraying himself as a 'professional' general, in contrast to his opponents, whom he characterized as amateurish aristocrats (Erdkamp 2010: 291).

After his election, Marius was authorized to recruit further troops to supplement those already serving in Numidia. He called for volunteers from allies and veterans, but crucially also from those citizens too poor to meet the minimum property qualification, the so called *capite censi*, or 'head count'. According to the Roman historian Sallust (Gaius Sallustius Crispus), Marius was inundated with eager volunteers, who he pledged to arm and equip using money from the Roman treasury, and who were attracted by a legionary's regular pay, and the hope of a share of the booty that Marius' victory would bring. Sallust records that many members of the elite felt that Marius looked for volunteers from the poorest classes to gain their support for his political ambitions: as the poor had nothing, the elite feared they would owe Marius for everything (Sallust, *Bellum Iugurthinum* 86; Sage 2008: 238–39; Keppie 1984: 61–62). Marius took his expanded force to Numidia, and through a combination of military success and treachery, captured Jugurtha and brought the war to an end.

As well as opening service in the legions to those previously too poor to join, Marius was responsible for several other military innovations. He

reduced the legions' reliance on the baggage train and compelled his soldiers to carry their own equipment and cook their own meals. This led to the legionaries' nickname, 'Marius' mules' (Plutarch, *Vit. Mar.* 13). In addition, Marius introduced a new form of *pilum* that would easily bend on contact with an enemy's shield (Plutarch, *Vit. Mar.* 25). The Roman writer Pliny the Elder (Gaius Plinius Secundus) recorded that Marius also dispensed with most of the traditional animal symbols of the legions – the eagle, wolf, minotaur, horse and boar – and made the eagle the sole standard (*Naturalis Historia* X.16). This provided the legions with a single focus for loyalty, and a single standard to defend in battle. Marius may also have reorganized the legions, removing the distinctions of position and equipment between the three ranks of legionaries. Certainly, by this time all legionaries carried short swords, large oval shields and two heavy javelins (Keppie 1984: 66–67). This change may have been a response to the fact that the ranks of the Roman Army were increasingly filled by the poorest citizens, and therefore the traditional distinctions of age and class in the legions no longer reflected their social composition (Erdkamp 2010: 291–92).

For centuries, the Roman Army had been accompanied in war by a roughly equal number of 'allied' troops (from the Latin *ala*, or 'wing'). These were provided by loyal communities from the rest of Italy, known as *socii*. Rome had concluded different treaties with these communities, but all contained the obligation to provide infantry soldiers, and often also cavalry, for the Roman Army whenever required. By the time of Marius' reforms, these soldiers were probably equipped like Roman legionaries but were organized into their own units, known as cohorts (*cohortes*), which were often led by their own officers.

Relief carving of infantry combat from a monument celebrating the Julii family in Glanum. Though this artistic representation does not accurately depict the appearance of legionaries during Caesar's civil war, several contemporary helmet styles are shown. The transverse crest of the helmet worn by the standing figure third from left probably denotes he is a centurion. (Albert Ceolan/De Agostini Picture Library via Getty Images)

4

10

5

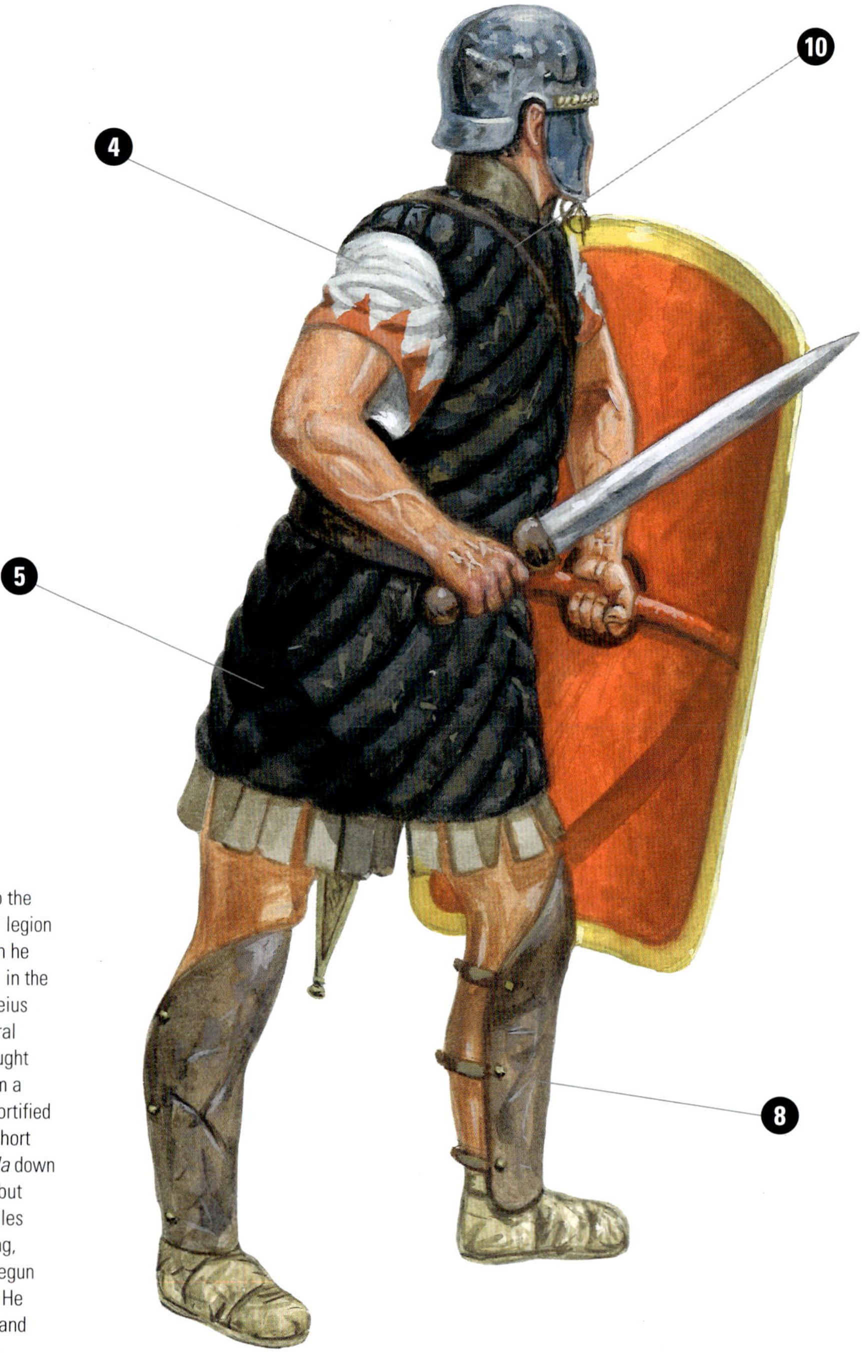

This recent recruit into the
Spanish 'home-grown' legion
is 20 years old. Though he
has been campaigning in the
army of Gnaeus Pompeius
'the Younger' for several
months, he has not fought
in a battle before. From a
high point below the fortified
town of Munda, his cohort
has been launching *pila* down
into the enemy ranks; but
after exchanging missiles
for much of the morning,
the Caesarians have begun
to advance up the hill. He
has raised his *scutum* and
drawn his *gladius* and,
terrified, prepares to meet the
onslaught.

8

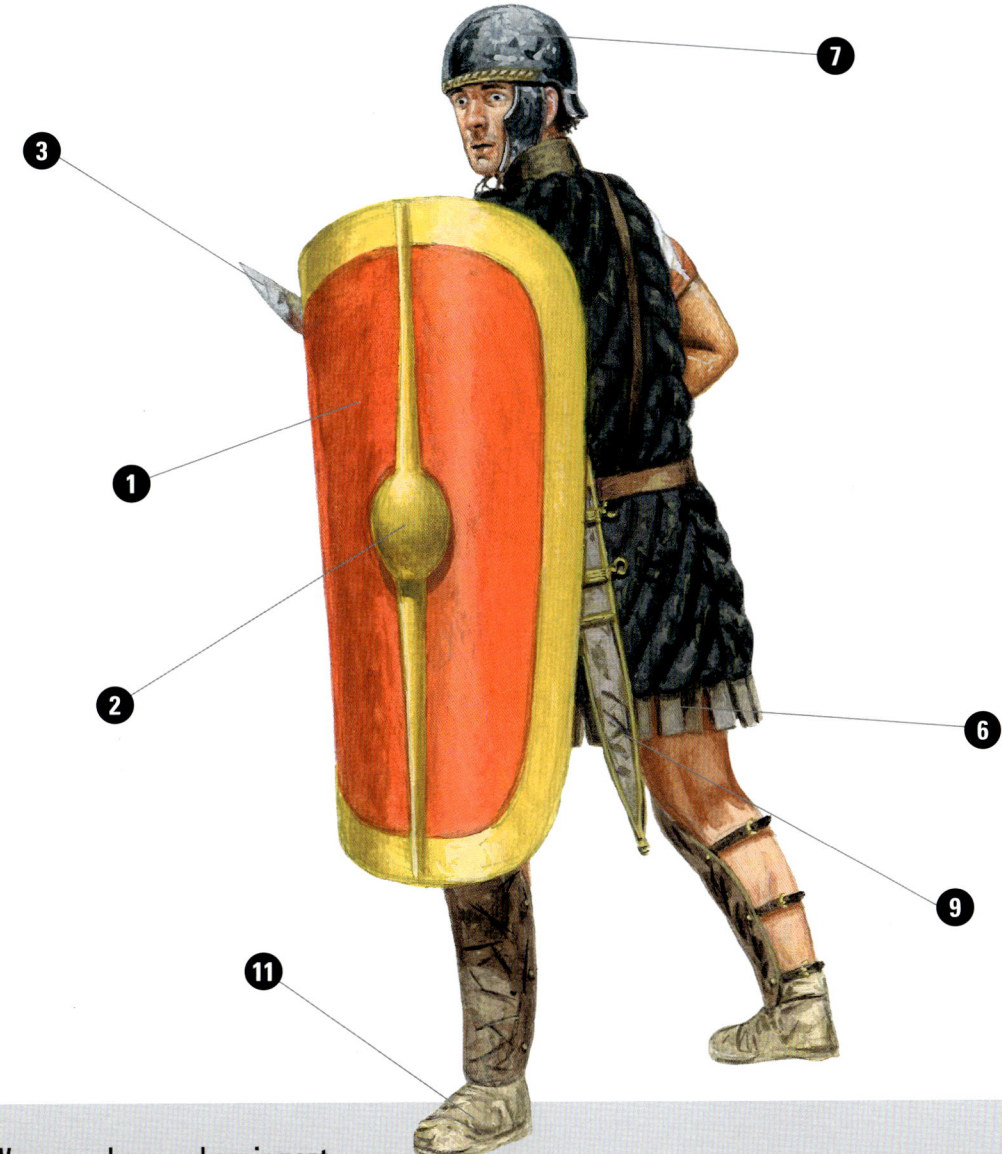

Weapons, dress and equipment

The weapons and equipment of this Spanish legionary owe as much to local traditions as Roman practice. His new shield (*scutum*; **1**), so far unscarred by enemy weapons, has an unusual trapezoid shape, which may be derived from Iberian or Celtiberian designs. Like the standard legionary shield, the front is reinforced with a long wooden spine that swells into a boss (*umbo*; **2**) in front of the horizontal handgrip, which as well as strengthening the *scutum*, turns it into an offensive weapon. After punching an enemy with the boss, the young recruit will jab and thrust at their face and abdomen with the long, tapering point of their short sword (*gladius*; **3**), of the type the Romans adopted from Spanish patterns in the previous century.

The sleeves of his woollen tunic (*tunica*; **4**) are decorated with geometric designs, and his torso and abdomen are protected by two layers of organic armour (*loricae*; **5**): beneath a thickly padded woollen jerkin, he wears a leather garment with a stiff collar that rises to protect his neck and throat, and a skirt of leather strips (*pteryges*; **6**), which allows his legs full freedom of movement. He is grateful for the strength of his iron helmet (*galea*; **7**) that has cheek pieces to guard his face but which leave his ears and eyes free. His leather greaves (*ocreae*; **8**) are scratched from marching through the rocks and undergrowth of the valley of the Baetis River. Following local custom, his scabbard (**9**) is suspended from a leather baldric (**10**) at his left hip, rather than the right as was more usual for Roman legionaries, and he wears soft leather boots (*calcei*; **11**).

The obligation to provide troops was a significant onus for the *socii*, the poorer independent farmers of which faced the same economic hardship as their counterparts in Roman territory. Yet they did not enjoy the same political or economic rights. The allied communities campaigned for equal status. This reached a crisis in 91 BC, when several broke away from their alliances with Rome and formed their own confederacy, called *Italia*. Rome quickly recruited fresh legions and marched against the breakaway *socii*. The brutal conflict that followed has become known as the 'Social War' of 91–87 BC (Konrad 2010: 177–78). In early engagements, the Italians achieved several victories; but the Romans were able to build up and maintain a much larger army, assisted by foreign auxiliaries. In 90 BC the Roman senate passed a law granting citizenship to those allied communities that had not broken with Rome, or had ceased fighting. Many of the allies accepted the offer. The few that continued to resist were defeated one by one. The last was forced to surrender in 88 BC, and soon after the Romans bestowed citizenship on all of Italy south of the Po River (Keppie 1984: 68; Konrad 2010: 178).

The extension of citizenship to the allied communities had significant consequences for the Roman Army, and the future of the Republic itself, for legionary soldiers could now be recruited from anywhere in Italy. After the Social War, not only were legionaries likely to be completely reliant on their military pay for their subsistence, but were also drawn from communities far from Rome, with whom many had recently been at war. They therefore owed the Republic no allegiance. The Roman senate's reluctant incorporation of the *socii* into the citizen body to end the Social War put the Republic at risk from a new threat: a military coup led by one of its own commanders at the head of an army of alienated and self-interested soldiers. In 88 BC, just as the last Italian communities submitted to Rome, this is exactly what happened.

War broke out in Asia Minor (modern-day Turkey). Mithridates VI Eupator, the king of Pontus (r. 120–63 BC), invaded the neighbouring kingdoms of Bithynia and Cappadocia and the Roman province of Asia. Mithridates ordered the massacre of Roman and Italian citizens, including women and children, across Asia Minor. As many as 80,000 were killed. He then advanced into Greece (Konrad 2010: 178–79). The Roman senate declared war and gave the task of removing Mithridates to the newly elected consul, Lucius Cornelius Sulla, an able general who had helped to capture Jugurtha and fought with great distinction in the Social War. Before Sulla could leave for the East, however, his political opponents in Rome succeeded in replacing him as general with Marius. Sulla immediately turned to his troops, who were massed near Rome in readiness for the campaign. The soldiers were keen to fight in wealthy Asia Minor, from where there was a very good prospect of returning with booty. Sulla persuaded them that Marius intended to raise new legions for the fight against Mithridates, and that they should follow him to reclaim what was rightfully theirs. Sulla marched on Rome with six legions of disgruntled soldiers. All but one of his officers fled, however, unhappy at leading a Roman army against Rome itself (Keppie 1984: 70). When Sulla and his army reached the city, he declared Marius and his associates to be public enemies, settled affairs in his own favour and set off with his army to Greece to deal with Mithridates (Konrad 2010: 179–80). Sulla returned to fight, and eventually win, a brutal civil war.

Sulla's soldiers returned from Greece richer. They rewarded their commander with their loyalty in the ensuing civil war, and with political support afterwards, just as Marius' soldiers had done 20 years earlier. Sulla hoped to entrench that support. He set up a series of colonies, on land seized from communities around Italy that had opposed him during the civil war. Each colony was divided into small plots, which he awarded to his loyal veterans. Sulla was thus able to reward his soldiers, most of whom had joined the legions because they lacked any other means of subsistence, with enough land to make them financially independent. In return, he expected his newly settled veterans to serve him in the future and help quell any attempt by the communities around the colonies to resist Roman rule (Keppie 1984: 71). The promise of land to loyal veterans on the completion of their service became a major motivating factor for the recruitment of soldiers in the civil war of 49–45 BC, and those that followed.

In 58 BC, Julius Caesar took command of Roman forces in Gallia Cisalpina (modern-day northern Italy, between the Po and the Alps), Illyricum, and soon after also Gallia Transalpina, which stretched around the coast between the Alps and northern Hispania. He inherited four legions: VII, VIII, IX and X. In the decade of campaigning that followed, Caesar conquered the whole of Gaul, crossed the Rhine twice, and led two expeditions to Britain. This obviously required a much larger force. By 49 BC, when Caesar left his allotted province of Gallia Cisalpina and crossed into Italy, triggering civil war, he had increased his army to 12 legions (though two had been sent to Italy for a planned campaign against the Parthians).

Caesar recruited soldiers for his new legions himself. He attracted volunteers among Roman citizens from south of the Po, and from communities north of the river in Gallia Cisalpina, who enjoyed rights similar to those of some Italian *socii* before the Social War. Caesar appears to have ignored the fact that men from these communities (as non-citizens) were not legally eligible to join the legions. He may have assumed the right to grant citizenship to these Gallic troops. Caesar also recruited a 'militia' from settlements on the other side of the Alps. When he marched on the Apennine town of Corfinium (modern-day Corfinio, Italy) at the start of the civil war in 49 BC, Caesar reports in his *Commentaries* that he was joined by 22 cohorts of recruits from Gaul (*BCiv.* 1.18). It is likely that these units were later formed into a new 'Gallic' legion, Caesar's *legio V*, known as the *Alaudae*, or 'larks', possibly because they decorated their helmets with long feathers (Keppie 1984: 98).

Caesar's recruitment of so many legionaries from either side of the Po gave his army a unique and cohesive identity (Keppie 1984: 98). His troops originated from the same, relatively small area, far from Rome, and like those in the army of Sulla, owed the Republic no particular loyalty. Caesar's repeated military success in Gaul, however, and the wealth his victories generated for his soldiers, combined with his inspiring leadership style and powerful charisma, produced an unparalleled personal loyalty in his soldiers. Many of his legionaries served him for decades, and some went on to serve in the armies of his heir.

Despite the numbers of Roman citizens available, the emergency of civil war forced commanders to widen recruitment to all classes of men. At Brundisium (modern-day Brindisi, Italy), Pompey gathered shepherds and slaves to act as a cavalry screen to slow Caesar's pursuit (Caesar, *BCiv.* 1.24), and one of his officers, Lucius Cornelius Lentulus, briefly enlisted gladiators (Caesar, *BCiv.* 1.14). Another officer, Publius Attius Varus, levied two legions in Africa, probably from Roman colonists. Hispania was an important source of troops for both sides, as much of the war was fought there. Pompey's legates recruited thousands of Celtiberian and Iberian auxiliaries (Caesar, *BCiv.* 1.37), and the sources record the involvement of two local legions, known as the 'Colonials' and the 'Homebred'. The 'Colonials' was almost certainly composed of Roman colonists and their descendants, but the origin of the 'Homebred' is less clear; it may have been recruited from families of the local elite, who had been granted Roman citizenship for service to the Republic (Caesar, *BCiv.* 2.19–20; *BHisp.* 7).

Both sides strengthened their armies with foreign auxiliaries and allied troops, but also with allied 'legions'. The Romans had been training the armies of foreign allies in the use of their own weapons and tactics since the War with Hannibal, and several kingdoms surrounding Rome's foreign territory had incorporated legions equipped in the Roman manner into their own armies. The Numidian king Juba I (r. 60–46 BC), a friend and ally of Pompey, led his 'legions' against Caesar in Africa in 46 BC (*BAfr.* 59); and in Asia Minor, the Galatian ruler Deiotarus I (r. *c.*65–*c.*40 BC) lent his 'legions' to Caesar for the campaign against Pharnaces II of Pontus (r. 63–47 BC), son of Mithridates VI Eupator, in 47 BC. Deiotarus' 'legions' were subsequently incorporated into the Roman Army and formed part of the army of the emperors: *legio XXII*, known as *Deiotariana*, was stationed in Alexandria in Egypt until the early 2nd century AD (Pollard & Berry 2012: 28, 123–26).

During the civil war, many legionaries deserted Pompey and his officers for Caesar, and significant numbers ultimately fought for both sides. Soldiers deserted individually, in groups, and at times whole units left Pompey's armies: soon after Caesar entered Italy in 49 BC, 20 cohorts commanded by Lucius Domitius Ahenobarbus abandoned their general at Corfinium and joined Caesar (Caesar, *BCiv.* 1.17–23). Defeated and captured Pompeian troops were also given the opportunity to serve the victor. After the battle of Pharsalus (modern-day Farsala, Greece) in 48 BC, Caesar incorporated surrendered Pompeian troops into his own army, many of whom went on to fight in campaigns in Egypt and Asia Minor (Caesar, *BCiv.* 3.99; *BAlex.* 9). There are few accounts of legionary soldiers deserting Caesar's army. In 49 BC, one of Caesar's legates, Gaius Antonius – the brother of Mark Antony – was captured off the coast of Illyricum with 15 cohorts. Some of these troops were distributed among Pompey's legions (Caesar, *BCiv.* 3.4). During Caesar's campaign against Pompey's sons in Hispania in 45 BC, Aulus Valgius, the son of a senator, fled to the Pompeian camp to join his brother (*BHisp.* 13).

On enlistment, Roman legionaries swore an oath of allegiance to their commander, called a *sacramentum*. The oath was religious in nature, and bound soldiers to not desert their standards or general, to carry out their

duties in camp, and not to steal. If a new commander was appointed, soldiers would expect to swear a new oath (Sage 2008: 123–25). During the civil war, the sanctity of the *sacramentum* was clearly not always respected. After Domitius Ahenobarbus' soldiers deserted him at Corfinium, they were sent to Africa under Caesar's legate Curio. As the two sides lined up for battle, one of Pompey's officers, Sextus Quintilius Varus rode up and down the lines of Curio's legions and begged them to remember their first military oath, which they had sworn to Domitius. The deserters ignored him.

LEADERSHIP

During the Roman Republic, the Roman Army on campaign was commanded by an elected or appointed official, known as a *magistrate*. The most senior magistrates in the Republic were the two consuls, who were elected to serve for one year each. The consuls had two important powers: *imperium*, the right to command citizens in Rome and citizen soldiers in the military, and *auspicium*, which was the power to interpret the will of the gods on behalf of the Republic (North 2010: 263). Immediately below the consuls were the *praetores*, who also possessed *imperium*. In the early centuries of the Republic, the two consuls would command Rome's army, and new legions would be raised by the consuls every year. From the mid-3rd century BC Rome regularly fought overseas, and armies had to stay in the field for years at a time. In these circumstances, the senate 'prorogued', or extended, the magistrates' *imperium* for one year or more, and they became *proconsules* or *propraetores*. With war came empire, and it soon became necessary to appoint additional magistrates with *imperium* to govern Rome's overseas territory, and campaign against the Republic's many enemies. From the late 2nd century BC, it was common practice for magistrates to be given a *provincia* (literally 'task') or 'province' overseas by the senate after their year in office came to an end (North 2010: 270). By the time of Sulla, consuls were prohibited from leaving Rome during their year in office, and from 52 BC, magistrates had to wait five years after holding office in Rome before taking command of a province (Keppie 1984: 78). A *propraetor*'s *imperium* was limited to the boundaries of his province. As soon as he left his allotted province, he gave up his *imperium* (Keppie 1984: 102).

The figure at left from the 'Domitius Anenobarbus' altar base, now in the Louvre Museum in Paris, France, represents a Roman officer of the late 2nd century BC, but officers of both sides in Caesar's civil war probably wore similar clothing and equipment. This may be a military tribune, a junior staff officer on campaign, and his expensive armour and dress owe much more to Greek military fashions than Roman. His helmet is of the Italo-Corinthian type, which retained only as decoration the eyeholes and nose guard of the Corinthian helmets worn by Greek hoplites. This style of helmet was almost exclusively worn by Roman officers in this period. Unlike legionaries, whose armour was made of ring mail, this tribune wears a so called 'muscle cuirass' made of copper alloy, or possibly leather, which is shaped to represent the human torso, over a fabric garment with a 'kilt' of linen strips, known as *pteryges*. Metal greaves protect his lower legs, and his rank is signified by the sash around his waist. His *paludamentum*, or cloak, was worn by high-ranking Romans on campaign in place of the *toga*. (Jastrow/Wikimedia/Public Domain)

A relief carving from Osuna, Spain, showing a Roman trumpet player. The trumpet was used for signalling by the Roman Army throughout its history. At Thapsus, when an overenthusiastic trumpeter sounded the command to charge, Caesar's legionaries began to assault Scipio's camp against Caesar's orders (*BAfr.* 82). (Universal History Archive/Universal Images Group via Getty Images)

Roman *proconsules* and *propraetores* were assisted by senior officers known as legates (*legati*), whom they appointed directly. The main role of the legate was to act as deputy commander. He could command one or more legions and auxiliary forces independently (in this period, individual legions had no permanent commanding officer), or command part of an army in a major battle. Legates were also often responsible for running a camp during winter,

Though this relief carving from the gravestone of a Roman centurion, Titus Calidus Severus, dates from the 1st century AD, the equipment shown is the same as that worn by centurions during Caesar's civil war: a helmet with a transverse crest, greaves (lower leg armour) and a cuirass. The cuirass shown here may be a representation of 'scale' armour, made of rows of metal plates sewn onto a textile backing, or it may be intended to represent some kind of quilted fabric body protection. (DEA/A. DAGLI ORTI/De Agostini via Getty Images)

and for the administration of part of a province. During his campaign in Gaul, Caesar had ten legates, and they were essential to his ability to control his forces over a wide geographical area (Keppie 1984: 99–100). Caesar's most trusted legate was Labienus, whom he left in command of the army in Gaul during his expedition to Britain in 54 BC. Pompey governed his Spanish provinces through two of his own legates, Marcus Petreius and Lucius Afranius, while he carried out other duties in Rome.

Each legion was staffed by several more junior officers, called military tribunes (*tribuni militum*). These were usually young men from elite Roman families, who were required to serve in the legions as part of their political careers, though some may have been interested in pursuing a career more focused on military command. Military tribunes appear to have fulfilled a predominantly administrative and political role, rather than a tactical one. While many carried out their duties effectively, others proved more of a burden (Keppie 1984: 98). Commanders included these young men on their staff because of their political connections, or because their families may have lent or donated funds to the campaign.

ARMY ORGANIZATION

The main fighting strength of the Roman Army was its heavy infantry, organized into legions of 4,800 men (in practice, units rarely operated at full strength due to death, wounds, illness and desertion). Each legion was divided into ten cohorts of 480 men, which in turn were divided into six centuries (*centuriae*) of 80 men each. The cohort was the main tactical unit of the Roman Army in the 1st century BC. In his *De Bello Civili*, Julius Caesar often specifies the number of cohorts present, even when the number represents several legions (e.g. *BCiv.* 1.15). Previously, each legion had been divided into smaller tactical units, called maniples (*manipuli*; literally 'handfuls'), which were formed by two centuries of soldiers from the three lines of the old legionary system: *hastati*, *principes* or *triarii*. The first two lines, *hastati* and *principes*, formed centuries of 60 men, and maniples of 120. The *triarii* formed centuries of only 30 men, and maniples of 60. A cohort was thus formed by the combination of three maniples, one of each line of legionaries. This organization was retained in the new system, to the extent that the centurions, the ranks of the officers who commanded each century, were named after the three old lines (Keppie 1984: 63–64).

It is not clear precisely when the change from maniple to cohort took place, but it is likely to have been a gradual process, and the cohort and maniple may have been in use at the same time. Some historians credit Marius for this reorganization (though no ancient source does so), because after he effectively removed the minimum property qualification for joining the legions, recruits were increasingly drawn from the poorest classes: the old distinctions of age and wealth, and therefore the three different lines, quickly became redundant, and all legionaries began to be equipped in the same way (Keppie 1984: 6; Sage 2018: 221). The cohort had in fact existed for many years, as it was the standard unit for the infantry of the Roman allies, or *socii*. Each allied cohort contained 400–600 men, probably the number of troops that an allied town could easily muster, and was led by a local officer, known as a *praefectus* or 'prefect'. Ten allied cohorts formed an *ala* or 'wing', the equivalent of a Roman legion, which was commanded by a Roman officer (Sage 2008: 127). Roman generals might have recognized the strength and flexibility of the individual allied cohorts on the battlefield and reorganized their legions in a similar fashion: units of approximately 500 men were far more potent than maniples of only 120, and it was much easier to communicate orders to ten units instead of 30 (Sage 2008: 200). Cohorts were also large enough to operate independently, but not so large as to become unwieldy.

Each of the six centuries in a cohort was led by a centurion. These men belonged to a 'class' of officers, rather than a particular rank, and there was a great distinction in pay and prestige between the most senior of the six centurions in a cohort, and the most junior, as there was between the senior centurions of each of the ten cohorts in a legion. The position of senior centurion of the first cohort, the *primus pilus,* or 'first spear', was very prestigious. In the absence of any evidence of a rank of 'cohort commander', it is most likely that this role was assumed by the most senior centurion in the cohort (Sage 2008: 202). Centurions progressed through the ranks as positions became available, but could also be promoted to more senior roles in newly recruited legions.

The century, ideally composed of 80 men, was retained from the manipular system but probably became more of an administrative unit. Legionaries were grouped into a *contubernium*, or 'tent', of eight men who lived and cooked

This figure from an altar that once stood in the Temple of Neptune, known as the 'Altar of Domitius Ahenobarbus', represents a legionary of the late 2nd century BC, but his ring-mail armour, Montefortino-type helmet with long horsehair plume and curved, oval shield are like those carried by legionaries of both sides during Caesar's civil war. The curve of the shield, and the design of the horizontal handgrip, are clear. The shield was held with an overhand grip, and the inside of the hollow boss was lined with wool or horsehair to protect the soldier's hand when he thrust his shield at an opponent, or parried blows. (Jastrow/Wikimedia/ CC0 1.0)

By the time of Caesar's civil war, the cohort had become the main tactical unit of the Roman army. In theory, each cohort was composed of six centuries of 80 men each, giving a total unit strength of 480. Losses to death, wounds, illness and desertion meant, however, that cohorts rarely operated at full strength during the conflict. In his account of the battle of Pharsalus in 48 BC, after naming several key legions, Caesar recorded the strength of his army as 22,000 soldiers, divided into 80 cohorts, and that of Pompey as 47,000 soldiers, divided into 110 cohorts (*BCiv.* 3.88–89). Caesar's cohorts were therefore composed of an average of only 275 soldiers, and Pompey's of an average of 427. There is limited evidence of the way in which the cohort was deployed. At Pharsalus, Pompey arrayed his cohorts in ranks ten men deep (as shown here). A formation only six men deep may have been more usual, however, because the cohort would present a front rank 80 men wide, which was the strength of a century, and the six centuries may have fought one behind the other. Each century was led by a centurion (**A**) and was represented by a standard (*signum*) carried by a *signifer* (**B**). Orders were communicated to the troops of the cohort by a trumpeter, or *cornicen* (**C**). There may have been only one *cornicen* in each cohort, as shown here, or perhaps one in each century. There is no evidence for a rank of cohort commander. The most senior centurion in a cohort may have commanded the unit in battle, possibly from the right side of the front rank (Sage 2018: 222–23).

together, forming a strong bond (Sage 2018: 222). Eight *contubernia* made up a century. A legionary identified himself within his cohort by the name of his centurion, who was responsible for handing out pay and maintaining discipline. Each century carried its own standard.

The legion was the main logistical unit of the Roman Army, but increasingly also became the focus for soldiers' loyalty and identity. When the Roman Army still functioned as a citizen militia, new legions were raised almost every year, and were disbanded when the campaigning season finished. Though individual soldiers may have served for several years, their units were renewed every year or two, so they never formed a particular tie to any legion. As the Roman Empire grew, and armies were kept in the field for years at a time, legions began to take on their own unique identities, as the soldiers within them built strong bonds based on their shared experiences on campaign. Marius' reform of legionary standards also gave each legion a single focus for loyalty and identity in the form of their 'eagle'. Julius Caesar fostered this development of 'legionary identity'. He was particularly fond of *legio X*, which was already serving when he assumed command of the Gallic provinces in 58 BC. He repaid the men of *legio X* for their bravery and loyalty by treating them as an 'elite' unit, and gave them the nickname of *Equestris*, or 'the knights', after several of them accompanied him on horseback to a parley with a Gallic chieftain (Pollard & Berry 2012: 26). Caesar's *legio V*, the *Alaudae*, had a particularly strong unit identity because they were recruited from the same area of Gaul. Several of Caesar's legions from the Gallic campaign and civil war, including *legio V* and *legio X*, were still in existence at the end of the 1st century BC, and formed part of the permanent army of the first emperor, Augustus.

At the same time as the cohort replaced the maniple in the legions, two other major changes in the organization of the Roman Army occurred. The Roman light infantry, and the Roman and Italian cavalry, disappeared, and were replaced by foreign auxiliary troops. At least until the war against Jugurtha, the poorest and youngest Roman citizens in the Army would join the *velites*, who wore no armour and formed a screen of skirmishers in front of the legions. After this, our sources contain no reliable references to the *velites*. It is possible that the *velites* were abolished by Marius, as part of his other reforms, but they were most likely absorbed into the legions for the same reason that the three ranks of *hastati*, *principes* and *triarii* fell out of use (Sage 2008: 204–06). By the time of the civil war of 49–45 BC the light-infantry role in most Roman armies was carried out by foreign troops. Some Mediterranean communities had been providing specialist soldiers to the Roman and other armies for centuries, such as archers from Crete, slingers from the Balearic Islands and fast light cavalry from Numidia. Caesar inherited a contingent of these troops when he arrived in Gaul in

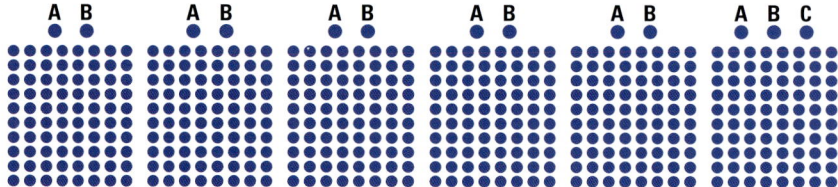

58 BC, but he did not retain them (Keppie 1984: 100). Despite relying heavily on foreign cavalry, Caesar made little use of non-Italian infantry during the civil war. By contrast, the armies of Pompey and his associates were reinforced by huge numbers of troops from his allies in Greece, Asia Minor and northern Africa.

In the early centuries of the Republic, the wealthiest citizens, the *equites*, or 'knights', formed the cavalry for the Roman Army. By the 2nd century BC, only those members of the equestrian class who wanted to pursue a political career (for which military service was essential) volunteered, and they normally served as military tribunes. Most of the cavalry was provided by Rome's Italian allies. At the beginning of the 1st century BC, however, as the *velites* disappeared, so do references in the sources to Roman and allied cavalry (Sage 2008: 206–07). From this point, the cavalry arm of the Roman Army was provided solely by foreign allies, predominantly Numidians, Gauls and Germans (Keppie 1984: 79). The cause of this change is not clear. It may simply be that Roman commanders found foreign horsemen to be more effective, or there may be an economic explanation: it was probably less costly to employ foreign auxiliaries rather than Italian cavalrymen, who would have expected higher pay than their legionary equivalents, and a contribution towards the maintenance of their horses.

WEAPONS AND EQUIPMENT

The Roman legions were heavy infantry. Legionaries lined up for battle in disciplined ranks and fought in close order. Their main offensive weapons were a heavy javelin, a short sword, and often also a dagger (*pugio*). For defence, legionaries were equipped with a large, curved shield that covered the body from shoulder to knee; a metal helmet, normally of copper alloy; and most likely some kind of body protection or armour, such as an iron ring-mail tunic, or garments manufactured from organic materials such as leather or felt. Under their armour, soldiers would have worn a short-sleeved tunic of wool or linen, that reached to the mid-thigh and was gathered at the waist with a leather belt, and a woollen cloak over the top in cold weather. Footwear, either open sandals or boots, was made from leather, with soles studded with iron nails.

Unfortunately, the evidence for the appearance of Roman legionaries during the late Republic is lacking. There are few extant items of militaria, such as swords or helmets, and very few visual representations of

During the mid-1st century BC, a Roman legion included ten cohorts, each with six centuries of 80 men. A legion at full complement, therefore, was 4,800 men strong, but casualties in battle, and losses from wounds, illness and desertion often reduced the number of soldiers considerably. Caesar's *legio IX* was so depleted by the fighting at Dyrrachium in 48 BC that at Pharsalus he combined the surviving legionaries with *legio VIII* to form a new unit. In battle, the cohorts were usually deployed in three lines, the so called *triplex acies* formation. Four cohorts formed the front line (**A**) supported by a second line (**B**) of three cohorts. The remaining three cohorts remained in reserve in the third line (**C**). There was probably a gap left between each cohort, and between the three lines, to allow cohorts to move forward to reinforce the legionaries in front, or to replace them when they became exhausted. The division of the legion into cohorts gave the Roman Army enormous flexibility, and generals often deployed their cohorts very differently to suit the circumstances of each battle. At Pharsalus, Caesar took one cohort from each legion and formed them into a fourth line on his left wing to counter Pompey's cavalry (Caesar, *BCiv.* 3.89); and at Thapsus, Caesar divided the cohorts of his *legio V* into two to form a fourth line behind each wing, opposite Scipio's elephants (*BAfr.* 81). Lucius Afranius deployed his five legions at the battle of Ilerda (modern-day Lerida) in Spain in 49 BC in only two lines, because he had sufficient auxiliary cohorts to form a third line of reserves. Opposite, Caesar arrayed his legions in the usual 4–3–3 formation (Caesar, *BCiv.* 1.83).

This scene from the base of an altar that once stood in the Temple of Neptune in Rome was probably carved in the late 2nd century BC. Now in the Louvre Museum, it shows two Roman legionaries and a Roman cavalryman preparing to take part in a religious ritual. All three figures wear ring-mail armour over their tunics, and the detail of the shoulder reinforcements can be seen. The legionaries' helmets are of the Montefortino type, with flowing horsehair plumes, which were still popular at the time of Caesar's civil war. The cavalryman wears a Boeotian helmet, a style adopted from the Greeks that mimics a soft, wide-brimmed hat. The legionaries carry large, oval shields, with long 'barleycorn' reinforcing spines, and oval *umbones*. It is not certain when the oval shield was replaced by the rectangular shield well known from images of Roman legionaries from the 1st century AD onwards. It is possible this change took place during the mid- to late 1st century BC, and that both types may have been in use during Caesar's civil war. (Jastrow/Wikimedia/CC0 1.0)

contemporary soldiers in paintings or sculpture, particularly in comparison with the Principate period, from the early 1st century AD onwards. The Roman Republic did not produce bombastic victory monuments in the style of the columns of the emperors Trajan (r. AD 98–117) or Marcus Aurelius (r. AD 161–180), which were decorated with hundreds of images of Roman soldiers and their defeated enemies. It was very unusual during the Republic for Roman men to be depicted on their gravestones as soldiers, even though they may have spent most of their lives serving in the Army, because legally, legionary service was still temporary. Under the emperors, however, the Army became a permanent institution, and soldiers served for at least 25 years. They increasingly reflected their 'military identity' in their funerary portraits, which provide invaluable evidence of soldiers' clothing and equipment. Literary sources also provide few details, because in most cases authors would have assumed their contemporary readership knew what soldiers looked like.

During the civil wars, there would have been little if any difference in the clothing and equipment carried by the legionaries of the two sides. To distinguish between themselves, some legionaries probably wrote the name of their commander on the front of their shields, and possibly also the number of their legion (*BAlex.* 58). There would, however, have been a great deal of variety evident in the weapons and armour of individual soldiers within each unit. There were no 'standard' patterns for the manufacture of military equipment, such as helmets or swords, and most items would have been produced locally whenever required. Metal goods were very valuable, so weapons or pieces of armour would have been kept for many years, and probably passed down to later generations of soldiers in the same family or traded within the legions. A

FAR LEFT
This 1st century BC statue, known as the 'Warrior of Mondragon', is part of the collection of the Musée Calvet in Avignon, France. Though the figure probably represents a Celtic tribesman, the construction of the shield visible here is like those carried by Roman legionaries. The shield is made from a 'plywood' formed from several layers of thin planks, laid side-by-side in different directions, and is reinforced with a long 'barleycorn' spine, carved from wood. A metal *umbo* or 'boss' covers the hole for the handgrip on the rear, which is held in place by rivets driven through butterfly-shaped extensions. The boss was used by Roman legionaries to strike an opponent, to push him off balance, before the soldier stabbed with his short sword, or *gladius*, at their belly, chest or face. (DEA/A. DAGLI ORTI/ De Agostini via Getty Images)

LEFT
This statue may represent a Celtic warrior from the 1st century BC, or perhaps a soldier of the auxiliary cavalry of the Roman Army of the Early Principate. Whoever this man was, the image he has left behind is one of the most useful sources for the construction of the ring-mail armour worn by Roman soldiers during this period. Note the shape of the shoulder reinforcements, which appear to be edged with leather, and the curved buckles and studs to hold them in place. The design of the studded belt and 'D'-shaped metal buckle are also clearly depicted. (Chris Hellier/Alamy Stock Photo)

1st century AD helmet found in Britain, for example, had the names of four different soldiers engraved inside it. Legionaries would also have improvised equipment from whatever was available. At Dyrrachium (modern-day Durrës, Albania) in 48 BC, Caesar's men fashioned extra body protection from animal hides and felt to protect against Pompeian arrows (Caesar, *BCiv.* 1.44), and Pompey's troops reinforced their helmets with woven wicker 'baskets' to fend off slingstones (Caesar, *BCiv.* 1.63).

The Roman legions regularly employed artillery during sieges, both to defend fortifications and to attack them. It was rare for artillery to be used in open battle because the individual machines were heavy and difficult to manoeuvre: most were probably constructed in place as required. The most common artillery piece used during the civil wars was a two-armed torsion catapult, known as a *ballista*, which could propel round stones, or wooden bolts tipped with pyramid-shaped metal points. *Ballistae* were built in many sizes. The largest were used to throw heavy stones long distances to destroy walls and buildings. The smallest bolt-throwing catapult was known as a *scorpio* and was used against soldiers. *Scorpiones* were surprisingly accurate. A bolt discharged from a *scorpio* from the walls of Leptis (modern-day Lemta, Tunisia) during the Thapsus campaign in 46 BC, struck a cavalry commander, passed through his armoured torso, and pinned him to his horse (*BAfr.* 29).

Dyrrachium

10 July 48 BC

BACKGROUND TO BATTLE

Caesar's arrival in Italy spread terror throughout the peninsula. In January 49 BC, Pompey had only two legions in Italy to resist Caesar's advance, both of which had recently been part of Caesar's army and thus could not be relied upon. Pompey had already begun to recall his veterans and to levy fresh troops; but, as he expressed in a letter preserved in the correspondence of the Roman orator and statesman Cicero (Marcus Tullius Cicero) with his friend Titus Pomponius Atticus, these recruits would be no match for Caesar's experienced legions (*Att.* 8.12). One senator mocked Pompey by reminding him of a boast he once made that he only needed to stamp his foot on the ground to produce an army in Italy (Plutarch, *Vit. Pomp.* 60).

Pompey decided to withdraw from Rome, and ultimately from the whole of Italy. He wrote to the consuls and proconsuls, asking them to muster all available forces at Brundisium, ready to cross to Dyrrachium. Pompey hoped to gather a huge army from his allies in Greece and the East, with which he could return to Italy and defeat Caesar.

Caesar's advance through Italy was astonishingly fast. Every town his forces approached surrendered without bloodshed, their citizens terrified of the consequences of

A coin of Pompey the Great depicting the Capitoline wolf suckling Romulus and Remus. (DEA/A. DE GREGORIO/ De Agostini/Getty Images)

resistance. After a few days, Caesar was joined by two more legions, XII and VIII, as well as 22 cohorts of soldiers from Gaul and 300 more cavalry. He marched for Brundisium, and arrived at the port city with six legions, having levied three legions of fresh troops on the way. The consuls had already sailed for Dyrrachium with most of their army, leaving Pompey in Brundisium with 20 cohorts. Caesar feared that Pompey might be trying to remain in the city, to keep control of both sides of the Adriatic Sea, so he decided to blockade the city from land and sea. After nine days of fighting at the mouth of the harbour, Pompey was delighted to see the ships that had transported the consuls and the rest of his army returning from Dyrrachium. Pompey managed to sail almost all his forces to safety. Plutarch remarked (*Vit. Pomp.* 63) that the withdrawal from Brundisium was among Pompey's most brilliant military achievements.

Caesar wanted to set off for Dyrrachium at once. He needed to prevent Pompey from reaching his allies in the East and building a new army – but Pompey had taken all the available ships, and Caesar could not afford to wait for vessels to arrive from further away. Six legions of Pompey's best soldiers remained in Hispania, commanded by two very experienced and able legates, Marcus Petreius and Lucius Afranius, who could also call upon vast reserves of local auxiliaries. Until Caesar dealt with this threat, Gaul and Italy lay exposed to attack from the West. He ordered ships to be gathered from all over Italy and marched for Hispania.

After a difficult campaign in which the soldiers of both sides suffered hunger and deprivation, Caesar defeated Pompey's Spanish legates. At the beginning of January 48 BC, he returned to Brundisium, where his army was assembling for the crossing to Dyrrachium; 12 legions were waiting for him, accompanied by all his cavalry. Caesar lamented the state of his army. Many of his legions were understrength due to losses on campaign in Gaul and Hispania, and the long march through Italy. Plutarch records (*Vit. Caes.* 37) how many of his older veterans travelled unwillingly to Brundisium, exhausted by years of constant soldiering. Poor weather around Brundisium

A simple copper-alloy helmet of the type now referred to as Coolus-Mannheim. Helmets of this type did not have cheek pieces and were held in place with a leather thong looped through holes in the rim. Though corroded, the attachment hole on this example is just visible, and the rear of the helmet is extended into a slight neck guard. As they were relatively cheap to manufacture, helmets like this one were probably in widespread use by legionaries of both sides during the civil war. (INTERFOTO/Alamy Stock Photo)

had brought disease. To make matters worse, Caesar had only managed to gather enough ships to transport 15,000 legionaries and 500 cavalry. To ferry his army across the Adriatic, his fleet would have to make more than one trip (Caesar, *BCiv.* 3.2).

Pompey had spent the past year gathering a diverse army. He had nine legions of Roman citizens: five he had brought with him from Italy; two were newly enrolled in Asia; one was made up of veteran soldiers who had settled in Crete and Macedonia; and the last was called the 'Twin' because it was formed from the remains of two legions of veterans from Cilicia in Asia Minor. The legions were brought up to strength with additional troops from around Greece, and Gaius Antonius' captured cohorts. Pompey also commanded 3,000 archers, 1,000 slingers and 7,000 cavalry from all over Greece and the East, including mounted archers from as far away as Commagene in Syria (Caesar, *BCiv.* 3.4). Pompey oversaw the training of his army at Beroea (modern-day Veria, Greece). Despite being nearly 60, he took an active role, participating in exercises on foot and on horseback, and throwing the javelin further than many much younger soldiers (Plutarch, *Vit. Pomp.* 64). A council of war was held at Beroea, at which Pompey was granted supreme command in the war against Caesar.

On 4 January, Caesar embarked the first of his troops, without their baggage and with minimum kit to allow the maximum number of soldiers on board. They reached the coast of Epirus (modern-day Albania) the next day. Caesar sent the ships back to Brundisium as soon as his soldiers had landed (Caesar, *BCiv.* 3.6–8). Pompey's fleet, commanded by Marcus Calpurnius Bibulus, a bitter political enemy of Caesar, attacked the empty ships, and established an effective blockade around the coast. Caesar's legates were unable to sail with Caesar's remaining forces, and he was unwilling to engage the enemy with his army so understrength. He decided to establish winter quarters near Apollonia, on the bank of the Apsus (now the Seman) River,

Helmets of the Montefortino type, like the one shown here, had been popular among soldiers of the Roman Army for at least two centuries before Caesar's civil war. Derived from Celtic designs, the pointed crown helped to deflect downward sword blows, and hinged cheek pieces provided protection for the face while leaving the ears and mouth exposed to allow soldiers to communicate in battle. Though the cheek pieces are missing from this example, the two rivets where they would have been fixed are clearly visible. The top of the helmet could be fitted with a holder for a plume made of horsehair or feathers. Legionaries probably lined their helmets with leather or fabric to improve the fit and make them more comfortable to wear. Padding would also help to cushion the wearer from blows to the head. Sadly, due to the organic nature of these materials, no such lining has survived. (Sepia Times/Universal Images Group via Getty Images)

and wait for the rest of his troops to reach him from Italy. Pompey set up his own winter camp on the other side of the river.

Caesar's legate, Mark Antony, eventually embarked the remaining legionaries and cavalry and joined Caesar in late April. With his army now complete, Caesar marched for Dyrrachium. He hoped either to capture the port and Pompey's arsenal of weapons, missiles and siege engines, or at least to cut off Pompey's access to them. Caesar led his army to the port by a circuitous route, hoping to disguise his intentions, but Pompey's scouts discovered the plan and Pompey rushed to intercept. Caesar just managed to reach the coast to the east of Dyrrachium as Pompey's column came into view from the south. Caesar ordered his men to set up camp and prepare for battle (Caesar, *BCiv.* 3.41). Pompey, dismayed at his failure to secure Dyrrachium, began to construct fortifications around a hill called Petra, which commanded a natural harbour. He mustered part of his fleet there, using the ships to bring food and supplies from Dyrrachium, which he could still reach by ship, and the areas of Greece and Asia under his control. He ordered his naval commanders to patrol the coast, to stop any supplies reaching Caesar by sea from Italy.

Caesar recognized that Pompey was planning a protracted campaign and set about securing his own food supplies. He sent legates to supportive cities in Epirus and Illyricum to empty their granaries, but they were a long distance away, and there was little grain to be had: the terrain was mountainous and unsuited to arable farming, so local communities relied on imports of wheat. Also, Pompey had a much larger cavalry contingent, and Caesar knew they could easily cut off any attempt by his men to bring in grain overland. Caesar decided to try to encircle Pompey's army (Caesar, *BCiv.* 3.43).

MAP KEY

1 After linking up with the forces brought over from Italy by Mark Antony, Caesar marches for Dyrrachium. As he approaches the city, Pompey's army arrives from the south. Caesar's men construct a camp, cutting Pompey off from Dyrrachium. Pompey occupies the hill known as Petra and builds his own camp.

2 Caesar fortifies several high points around Petra and joins them with a line of ditches and ramparts to enclose Pompey's army. Pompey responds with his own line of fortifications. Static warfare begins.

3 Caesar tries to break the stalemate by attempting to assault Dyrrachium. On the same day, Pompey mounts a major attack on one of Caesar's forts.

4 Acting on intelligence from two Gallic deserters from Caesar's army, Pompey leads his legions south to the incomplete section of Caesar's fortifications next to the shore. Light infantry assault the walls from the sea, supported by artillery on warships from Dyrrachium. Soldiers of Caesar's *legio IX* abandon their positions.

5 Marcellinus sends reinforcements from *legio IX*'s camp, but they are caught up in the rout from the walls. In the chaos, Pompey's men kill many of the soldiers of *legio IX*.

6 Caesar, alerted by smoke signals, arrives with most of his legions to find Pompey constructing a new camp outside his fortifications. Caesar discovers that one of Pompey's legions has occupied one of his old camps. Caesar attacks the camp with 33 cohorts and all of his cavalry. Half the Caesarian infantry assaults the gate and the rest advance around the wall surrounding the fort, accompanied by the cavalry.

7 After fierce fighting at the gate, Caesar's men take the fort. His remaining infantry and the cavalry mistakenly follow the wall towards the river. Realizing their error, they breach the wall and cross, just as Pompey's cavalry arrive. Caesar's men attempt to flee through the breach and are trapped. At the same time, Pompey arrives on the other side of the fort with five legions. Caesar's men inside the fort panic and try to escape through the narrow gate.

8 In the confusion that follows, many of Caesar's men are killed. Despite the rout, Pompey does not pursue Caesar's army. Caesar withdraws inland.

Battlefield environment

Pompey's legionaries built a continuous line of 24 forts around his camp at Petra, connected by ramparts and ditches that stretched more than 15 Roman miles (about 22.5km). Caesar's legionaries had to build an even longer line of fortifications of over 17 Roman miles (about 25km) to surround it fully.

The soldiers of both sides endured significant hardship. Caesar's men consumed their meagre wheat stocks in a short time, and could no longer make their own bread, the staple food of the Roman Army. Instead, they ate vegetables and even meat sourced from the mountain flocks of Epirus. Some soldiers dug up a root they found growing in low lying areas called 'chara'. When mixed with milk, it could be made into a loaf and eaten like bread (Caesar, *BCiv.* 3.48). According to Plutarch (*Vit. Caes.* 39), a few of Caesar's legionaries threw several of these loaves over the walls of a Pompeian fort and shouted to the defenders that if the earth continued to produce food for them, they would never abandon their blockade. When Pompey's soldiers showed him the food upon which their opponents were surviving, he declared with dismay that they were facing 'wild beasts' (Appian, *BCiv.* 2.61).

Pompey's men also suffered. Though there was plenty for the soldiers to eat, the area enclosed by their fortifications was too small to provide enough feed for their animals. Soon all but the cavalry horses had to be killed. It was also impossible to maintain adequate sanitation or find space away from encampments for the burial of corpses, and disease spread. Unlike Caesar's veterans, Pompey's troops were mostly unused

to building work, and the constant physical labour affected morale. To make conditions even more unpleasant, Caesar's men dammed or diverted all the streams flowing from the hills down towards the sea. As the blockade continued into summer, and the weather turned hot, Pompey's soldiers faced a serious shortage of fresh water. They resorted to digging wells in damp, marshy areas, which were unhealthy and far from their camps (Caesar, *BCiv.* 3.49).

The Roman amphitheatre in the modern-day city of Durrës, Albania (ancient Dyrrachium). Dyrrachium was an important city in the Roman Empire, as it was located at the head of the Via Egnatia, the main road east across northern Greece to Byzantium and the East. (Marica van der Meer/Arterra/Universal Images Group via Getty Images)

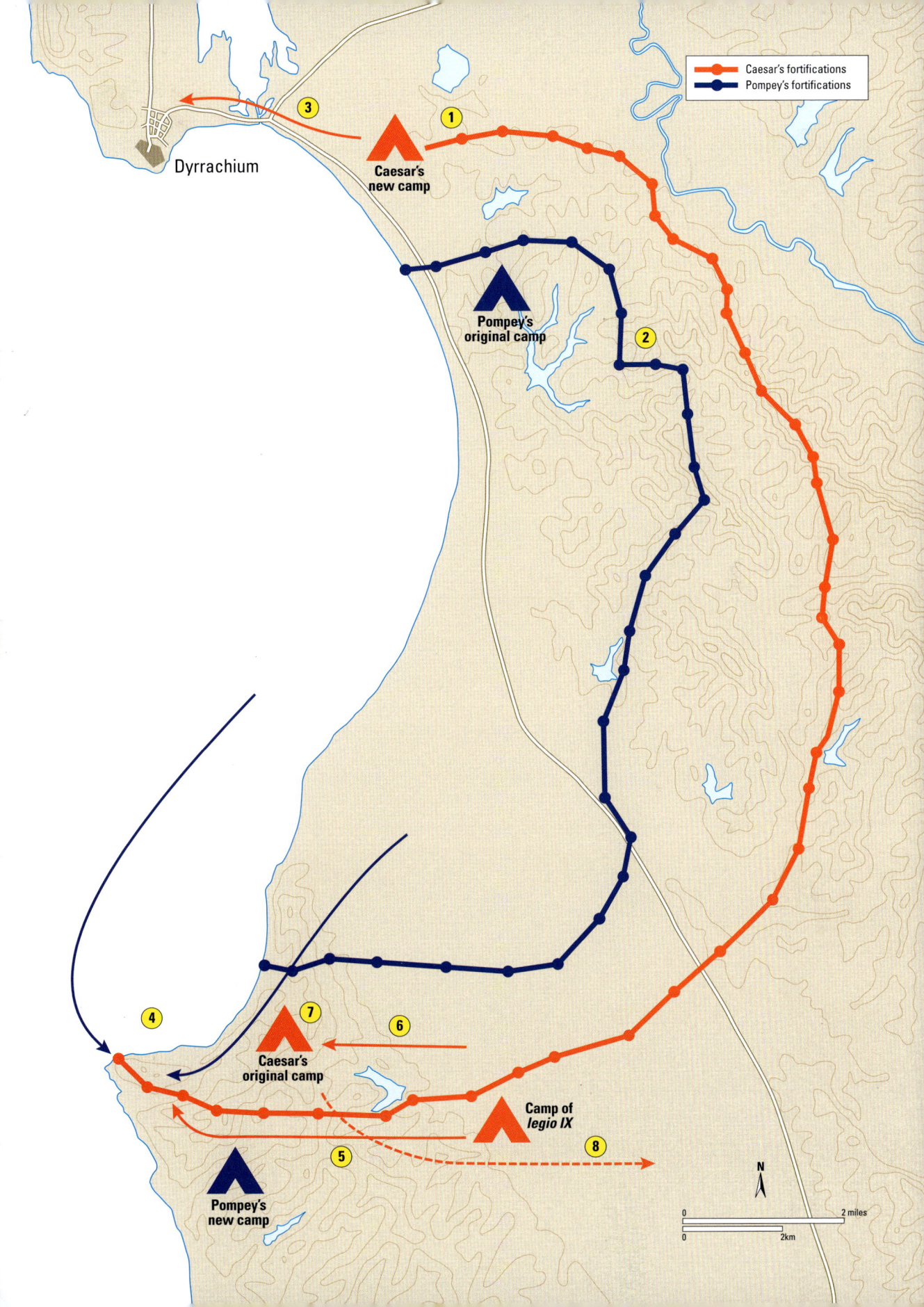

Caesar's fortifications

Pompey's fortifications

Dyrrachium

Caesar's
new camp

③

①

Pompey's
original camp

②

④

⑦

⑥

Caesar's
original camp

Camp of
legio IX

⑤

⑧

Pompey's
new camp

N

0   2 miles
0   2km

INTO COMBAT

Caesar's troops occupied several high points near Petra and began to construct fortifications upon them. They then joined these forts with lines of earth ramparts and ditches. In response, Pompey's soldiers built their own line of forts and entrenchments. Pompey tried to enclose as large an area as possible, to secure maximum access to grazing, and to stretch Caesar's forces thinly. Caesar's men had a much greater task, however, as they had to build a longer circuit of entrenchments but had fewer men to do so, and lacked access to the materials and equipment that Pompey could bring in by sea.

Pompey did not want to engage Caesar in open battle. Instead, he focused on preventing Caesar's legions from completing construction of their own fortifications with constant attacks, intending to exhaust the men and their supplies with minimal loss to his own. Wherever Caesar's soldiers tried to take a new position, or extend their fortifications, Pompey's allied missile troops would bombard them. The horrific barrage of arrows, stones and lead bullets launched from slings, as well as siege engines, wounded and killed many. Caesar's men found it impossible to both defend against these attacks and continue the construction work. To protect themselves while they worked, they fashioned extra armour from whatever they could find, such as animal hides, wool felt or quilts.

On one day, there were six major engagements (Caesar, *BCiv.* 3.53). Three took place at Dyrrachium, which Caesar may have decided to attack in response to an offer to betray the city that he received from someone inside (Appian, *BCiv.* 2.60). Unfortunately, the manuscripts of both Caesar's and Appian's accounts of the civil war are missing the sections that describe these encounters. It appears, however, that Caesar led the operation against Dyrrachium, as he left his legate Publius Cornelius Sulla, the nephew of Sulla the dictator, in charge of his camp (Caesar, *BCiv.* 3.51). The other three battles occurred along the fortifications. Pompey attacked Caesar's lines at several places at once, to split Caesar's forces, and stop reinforcements being brought in from other forts nearby.

Lead sling bullets were used by both armies during Caesar's civil war. Though the best slingers came from the Balearic Islands, Roman soldiers were also trained to use a sling to throw stones and clay and lead bullets long distances, and it was a popular hunting weapon. Many sling bullets have been found with inscriptions, either cast or scratched onto the surface. Some are derogatory remarks about the intended victim, while others record the unit that manufactured them. Sometimes sling bullets were used to send messages between two sides during a siege. (Heritage Art/Heritage Images via Getty Images)

Some of the circumstances of the first attack are lost in the same missing passages as the fighting at Dyrrachium. It seems that Pompey himself commanded a force of four legions in an assault on a fort manned by a single cohort of Caesar's *legio VI*. Pompey's archers and slingers maintained a ferocious hail of arrows and stones for many hours, and his legionaries made several attempts to breach the gate, the defence of which was led with astonishing bravery by a centurion called Cassius Scaeva (Suetonius, *Iul.* 68). Sulla came to their aid with two legions from Caesar's main camp, which easily drove off the attackers (Caesar, *BCiv.* 3.51).

Inside the fort the conditions must have been horrendous. Caesar reports that every soldier was wounded, and four centurions lost eyes. As proof of the ordeal they had suffered, after the fort was relieved, the defenders gathered up and laid out the arrows that had landed inside. They numbered 30,000. They also brought Scaeva's shield, which had been pierced 120 times (Caesar, *BCiv.* 3.53). Scaeva, though wounded in the eye, thigh and shoulder, survived (Suetonius, *Iul.* 68). Caesar rewarded him with a large cash bounty, and promotion to the rank of first centurion of the first cohort, or *primus pilus*. He also decorated all the other defenders, doubled their pay, and handed out generous gifts of food and clothing. Elsewhere, three cohorts of Caesar's legionaries led by an officer called Volcatius Tullus repulsed an assault by an entire legion of Pompey's troops. In another action, a unit of Germans killed several Caesarian soldiers in a hit-and-run raid in which none of the attackers were wounded (Caesar, *BCiv.* 3.52).

The stalemate continued. Conditions for Pompey's cavalry worsened, as their horses ate every remaining scrap of fodder within the blockaded area. His soldiers even stripped the leaves from trees and pounded up the roots of

These siegeworks at the Muséoparc d'Alésia, on the site of the siege of Alesia in Gaul (modern-day France), have been reconstructed based on evidence from archaeological excavations, and Caesar's detailed description in his *Bellum Gallicum* (7.72–74). The fortifications around Dyrrachium would have been built in a similar way, with a wide ditch in front of a high rampart. When Caesar's soldiers tried to escape from *legio IX*'s former fort, the narrow breach they had made became congested with panicking men, and many chose instead to leap from the 3m-high rampart. Those unfortunates who jumped first were trodden to death by their comrades, who clambered out of the trench over their bodies. (Prosopee/Wikimedia/CC BY-SA 3.0)

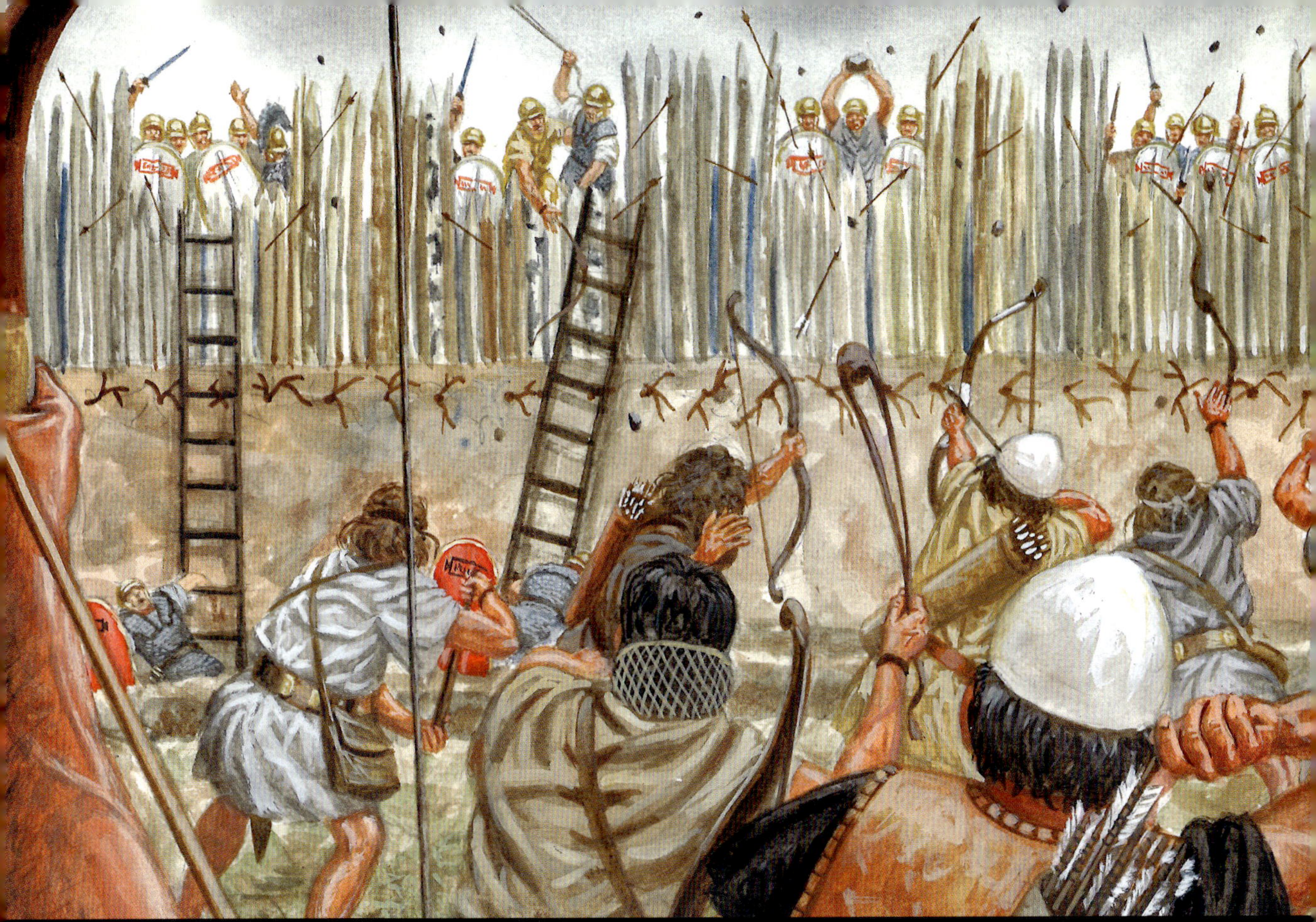

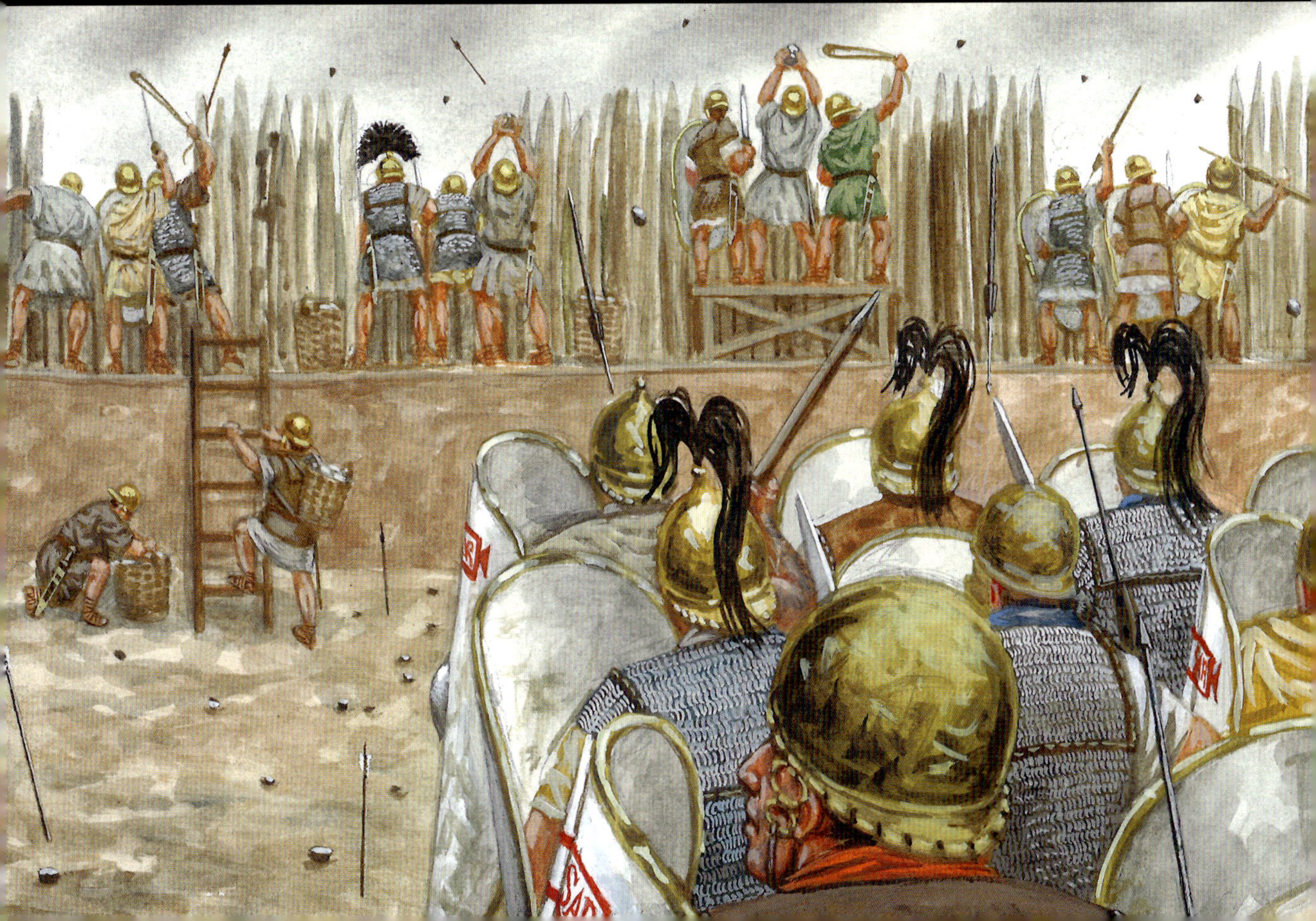

Confrontation at Dyrrachium

Pompeian view: Exhausted, a Cretan archer prepares to take aim at a Caesarian centurion defending the gateway into the enemy fort. The archer's arms and shoulders ache with pain as he draws back his powerful wood-and-horn bow, and releases what might be his hundredth arrow of the day. He prays that he will not be hit by a stone flung from the fort in response: unlike the legionaries, he has no helmet or armour to protect him. He is part of a large contingent of bowmen from Crete, Greece and Syria, who along with slingers from the Balearic Islands, have maintained a relentless barrage of arrows, stones and bullets into the fort for most of the day. It is now late afternoon, and from his left, the first ranks of a Pompeian legion are advancing for yet another assault on the gateway. They have already raised their *pila* and will cast them up at the defenders when their centurion gives the order.

Despite the hail of missiles, and several legionary attacks, the Pompeians have so far failed to dislodge the defenders from their rampart. Siege ladders from earlier assaults still lean against the defences, supported by the corpses of the brave men who tried to climb them. On the walls, Caesarian legionaries keep up their own fusillade of stones, or ready their *pila* to hurl as soon as the Pompeians come within range; others prepare to drop heavy rocks onto the attackers as they cross the ditch at the foot of the rampart. The rest huddle behind their *scuta*, clutching their short *gladii*, as stones and arrows rain down.

Caesarian view: The gateway must be held. As he sprints across the fort, a Caesarian legionary ignores the screams of a centurion hit in the eye by an arrow, and the pleas of a soldier trying to help him. Stones smash into helmets and clatter off armour; swishing arrows pierce raised shields or cut deep into unprotected flesh. The Pompeians are approaching for another assault, and the legionary has been ordered to leave his post on the rampart to aid Scaeva and the few men of his century still standing in the opening. Scaeva has led the defence at the gate all day, and as the legionary runs to help, he is thrilled to hear the valiant centurion's furious battle cry soaring over the clamour.

On the rampart, officers exhort the rest of the men to hold their positions. Soldiers scrabble to find stones and carry them in baskets up to the defences above: these small rocks dug from the ground within the fort are the only missiles available to the Caesarian slingers. Other soldiers get ready to drop larger rocks directly onto the attackers as they approach the base of the wall. As the legionary passes the wounded centurion, writhing and shrieking in a growing puddle of his own blood, he wonders: how much longer can our cohort hold on?

reeds for horse feed. In desperation, Pompey had to ship in fodder from as far away as Acarnania in Greece. Pompey knew that if his army could not break out, his horses would starve. Treachery provided salvation. Most of Caesar's cavalry were tribesmen from Gaul, loyal allies recruited during his long campaign to conquer that province; but two of these tribesmen, the brothers Roucillus and Egus, sons of Adbucillus, a chief of the Allobroges, deserted to Pompey after Caesar reprimanded them for embezzling from their fellow cavalrymen.

Though the slingers and stone throwers portrayed here on Trajan's Column date from the early 2nd century AD, they give a good impression of the equipment used during Caesar's civil war. (Conrad Cichorius/Wikimedia/Public Domain)

Marcus Calpurnius Bibulus

Pompey controlled a powerful fleet, with more than 500 warships, as well as other craft. He placed Marcus Calpurnius Bibulus in command. Bibulus had served as Caesar's fellow consul in 59 BC. When Bibulus tried to block Caesar's legislation granting land to Pompey's retiring veterans, Caesar humiliated him, and Caesar's violent supporters prevented him from carrying out his duties. As a result, Bibulus became Caesar's implacable enemy.

Bibulus was moored off Corcyra (modern-day Corfu, Greece), when he heard that Caesar's army was crossing to Dyrrachium in January 48 BC. His fleet arrived after Caesar's men had disembarked, but he captured 30 ships and set fire to them, burning their captains and crews. Bibulus was so determined to stop the rest of Caesar's troops from crossing that he slept aboard his ship, ready to sail at a moment's notice, despite the harsh winter conditions. His naval force quickly established an effective blockade of the ports and harbours along the coast of Epirus and Illyricum.

After landing, Caesar ordered one of his legions to patrol the coast and prevent Bibulus' ships from landing to take on water and supplies. Caesar's soldiers' control of the coast was as complete as Bibulus' blockade of the sea, and Bibulus' vessels had to return to Corcyra for provisions. On one occasion, when harsh storms kept the fleet from harbour, the crews were forced to collect dew that collected on the skins covering their ships (Caesar, *BCiv.* 3.15). Bibulus found the hardships too great, fell seriously ill and died (Caesar, *BCiv.* 3.18).

Bibulus commanded the Pompeian fleet from aboard a warship like that shown on this coin issued by Mark Antony in 33–31 BC (see also page 74). Life aboard such a vessel, crowded with rowers, sailors and marines, was very uncomfortable, particularly in poor weather. ((CNG Coins/Wikimedia/Public Domain)

This was disastrous for Caesar. Roucillus and Egus possessed intimate knowledge of Caesar's army, and crucially that his defences were incomplete where they neared the shore at their southern extent, furthest from Caesar's main camp near Dyrrachium. Caesar's men had built two parallel walls down to the sea but had not yet managed to join them, so the gap between them lay open to attack. Roucillus and Egus passed this devastating intelligence to Pompey, who acted immediately (Caesar, *BCiv.* 3.61). He ordered his legionaries to fashion extra coverings for their helmets from wicker and prepare material for constructing a rampart. That night, he loaded this onto a fleet of small, fast boats, along with archers, slingers and light infantry. Just after midnight, he marched at the head of 60 cohorts to the incomplete section of Caesar's fortifications and sent the boats along the shore at the same time, accompanied by warships from Dyrrachium (Caesar, *BCiv.* 3.62).

Caesar's entrenchments were manned at this point by soldiers of his *legio IX*, most of whom were camped near the shore. The commander of *legio IX* was the *quaestor* (junior magistrate) Publius Cornelius Lentilus Marcellinus. Both he and his men were completely unprepared for the scale of Pompey's dawn assault. As Pompey's legions approached the inner wall

Cassius Scaeva

The gallant exploits of the centurion Cassius Scaeva at Dyrrachium are recorded by several ancient writers. Caesar himself tells us (*BCiv.* 3.53) that Scaeva's shield was pierced 120 times, and that he rewarded Scaeva with an enormous gift of 200,000 *sesterces* (50,000 *denarii*; during the civil war, Caesar's legionaries were paid only 225 *denarii* per year), and promoted him from centurion of the eighth cohort to first centurion of the first cohort, or *primus pilus*, which made Scaeva the most senior centurion of the legion. The poet Lucan (Marcus Annaeus Lucanus), in his epic poem *Pharsalia* about the civil war, describes Scaeva's heroism in detail, and notes that he had risen from the ranks during Caesar's campaigns in Gaul (Lucan, 6.138–262). The Latin rhetorician Valerius Maximinus (fl. mid-1st century AD) in his collection of 'memorable deeds and sayings', records (3.2.23) that Scaeva had also fought with distinction during Caesar's invasion of Britain, though according to Plutarch (*Vit. Caes.* 16), this was a different soldier.

A man called Scaeva appears in the letters of the Roman orator Cicero, as a beneficiary of Caesar's generosity at the end of the civil war (*Att.* 13.23, 14.10). Considering the size of Scaeva's cash reward at Dyrrachium, it is plausible this is the same man. Perhaps the most captivating piece of evidence, however, is a lead sling bullet found at Perusia (modern-day Perugia, Italy). Octavian's army besieged the town in 40 BC during the civil wars between Octavian and Mark Antony. The sling bullet is engraved with 'SCAEVA L.XII' on one side and 'PR.PIL' on the other, standing for 'Scaeva, *primus pilus* of *legio XII*', presumably the officer who oversaw the making of the bullet. It is very tempting to assume this is the same Scaeva who fought with such distinction at Dyrrachium (Keppie 1984: 124–25), and that he went on to serve in the army of his heir. Centurions of the 1st century AD recorded the details of similarly long careers on their funerary monuments. Many such inscriptions survive, along with relief portraits illustrating the centurions' dress and equipment.

from the north, part of his light infantry and missile troops disembarked from the light craft behind the outer wall, surrounding *legio IX*. Pompey's legionaries brought up scaling ladders and attempted to overpower the soldiers defending the inner wall, as archers and slingers rained down a deadly fusillade of missiles, supported by artillery on the warships. Caesar's men had only stones to launch in response, but they rattled off the wicker helmet coverings of the Pompeians. While the defenders desperately sought to fend off the assault on the walls, Pompey ordered the rest of the light infantry to jump ashore in the gap between the two fortifications. They ran up the beach and caught the struggling *legio IX* from behind. Caesar's soldiers were overwhelmed and had no choice but to abandon the walls and flee (Caesar, *BCiv.* 3.63).

As soon as he heard about the assault, Marcellinus sent some of the remaining cohorts of *legio IX* up to the fortifications to assist. As the fresh troops met their retreating comrades, they too began to panic. Terrible confusion ensued, as soldiers from the walls tried to escape through the advancing lines of reinforcements, tripping over each other and hampering their withdrawal. Pompey's men pressed home their attack and cut down many of *legio IX*. In the throng, the standard bearer who carried the eagle of *legio IX* was mortally wounded. Before he collapsed, he handed over his standard to a fellow soldier. The eagle was saved but many members of the legion were not. All but one of the centurions of the first cohort were killed.

Mark Antony was in command of the nearest Caesarian fort. As soon as news of the assault reached him, he set out with 12 cohorts. When the soldiers of the beleaguered *legio IX* saw his column approaching, they rallied, and joined by Antony's men, checked Pompey's advance. At the same time, Caesar was alerted by smoke signals sent between the forts and arrived with more legionaries. He was appalled by the sight of Pompey's army outside of his cordon, freely gathering fodder along the shore (Caesar, *BCiv.* 3.65).

Caesar looked for a target for his own offensive. His scouts reported that Pompey had occupied a fortified camp abandoned by *legio IX* a few days earlier. Pompey's troops had moved in and built a second rampart around it to make the camp large enough for several legions and had extended one wall down to a nearby river, so soldiers could fetch water safely. The scouts told Caesar that a legionary standard had been erected inside the camp that morning, suggesting it had now been occupied by a single legion. Caesar left two cohorts to make a show of building his fortifications and set off to destroy the legion in the camp.

Caesar led a force of 33 cohorts, including the remains of *legio IX*, in two columns, accompanied by all his cavalry. They reached the camp without being observed and the left column immediately attacked. The Caesarians pushed the defenders back from the rampart, and stormed the gate, which was blocked by a massive wooden beam with spikes driven into it at all angles, known as a 'hedgehog'. After a short-lived but savage defence maintained by a Pompeian centurion called Titus Puleio, who had served Caesar in Gaul, the Caesarian legionaries cut through the hedgehog and poured through the gate (Caesar, *BCiv.* 3.67).

As fierce fighting continued in the camp, Caesar's right column and his cavalry advanced around the outside of the rampart, looking for a rear gate. They did not realize that they were following the line of the wall built by Pompey from the camp to the river. When they discovered their error, they breached the wall, which was undefended, and crossed over. The cavalry followed, just in time to spot Pompey's horsemen coming into view. Caesar's cavalry panicked, and not wanting to be trapped against the rampart, tried to retreat through the breach they had just made. The infantry of the right column, seeing the cavalry fleeing, also routed. A mass of terrified men and horses blocked the narrow breach, and many soldiers tried to leap off the rampart into the ditch below. The first to land were trodden to death as their comrades climbed over them to escape.

At the same time, Pompey arrived at the camp with five legions. The remaining defenders realized their commander had come to their aid, rallied around the rear gate of the camp, and charged the attackers. The Caesarians, when they saw Pompey's battle line forming up on one side of the rampart, and the flight of their own cavalry and right column on the other, turned and stampeded back through the front gate. Caesar himself tried to intervene. He urged the standard bearers to stop, so that the other men would rally around them, but they ignored him. Some threw away their standards (Caesar, *BCiv.* 3.69). Appian (*BCiv.* 2.62) and Plutarch (*Vit. Caes.* 39) record that Caesar grabbed the arm of a panicking soldier to restrain him. When the soldier raised his weapon to strike his general, Caesar's bodyguard cut the man's arm off at the shoulder with his sword.

Pompey did not pursue the routing Caesarians. His soldiers would have had to negotiate the same narrow gate and breach that trapped Caesar's men. Though in this one day of fighting at Dyrrachium Caesar lost 960 men, and 32 standards, his army had been saved from destruction. He abandoned the blockade and withdrew his army inland to continue the war.

Thapsus

6 April 46 BC

BACKGROUND TO BATTLE

After his forces' humiliating withdrawal from Dyrrachium, Caesar moved his army inland, towards Thessaly in central Greece. Pompey followed in pursuit with an enormous force of legionaries and allied troops. He tried to exhaust Caesar's men by denying them access to food supplies and fodder, but the other Roman senators in Pompey's army were impatient to bring Caesar to

Roman legionaries often named their equipment. Though this helmet probably dates from early in the 1st century AD, soldiers during Caesar's civil war may also have inscribed their helmets on the neck guard, where it was clearly visible. (INTERFOTO/Alamy Stock Photo)

A marble head of Cleopatra VII, found in Italy and now in the Altes Museum in Berlin, Germany. After his defeat at Pharsalus, Pompey sailed to Alexandria in Egypt to appeal to the young king Ptolemy XIII Theos Philopator (r. 51–47 BC), whose father Ptolemy XII Auletes (r. 80–58 BC and 55–51 BC) he had supported. Pompey arrived at Pelusium in the Nile Delta to find that Ptolemy was engaged in civil war against his sister Cleopatra. Ptolemy and his advisors argued about what to do with Pompey. Fearing the consequences of both supporting Pompey against Caesar, and rejecting Pompey's request for aid, they decided to do neither. They lured Pompey ashore and murdered him. When he discovered that Pompey had fled to Egypt, Caesar followed with a small force. Landing in Alexandria unaware of Pompey's violent death, Caesar tried to arbitrate between the two siblings, but ultimately sided with Cleopatra. After an arduous six-month campaign, Caesar defeated Ptolemy. He then joined Cleopatra for a six-month long cruise along the Nile River. (Louis Legrand/ Wikimedia/Public Domain)

battle. Pompey eventually relented and the two sides met at Pharsalus on 9 August 48 BC. Caesar won a comprehensive victory, and Pompey fled before the battle was even over. He eventually reached Egypt, where instead of finding sanctuary, he was murdered on 28 September. Caesar pursued Pompey but arrived at Alexandria in the Nile Delta after Pompey's murder. He became involved in a civil war in Egypt, which he settled after a brief but violent campaign, before marching to Asia Minor to deal with Pharnaces II of Pontus, the son of Mithridates VI Eupator whom Pompey had defeated 20 years earlier. Pharnaces had invaded his father's old territory and brutalized several Roman supporting communities. Caesar 'came, saw and conquered' Pharnaces at the battle of Zela on 2 August 47 BC, then returned to the west to confront his remaining Roman enemies.

Plutarch remarked (*Vit. Pomp.* 76) that Caesar's greatest achievement at Pharsalus was to bring Pompey to battle so far inland that he could gain no advantage from his enormous fleet. After the defeat of Pompey's army, this fleet remained intact. Pompey's surviving generals – including his father-in-law Scipio (Quintus Caecilius Metellus Pius Scipio Nasica); Caesar's former legate, Labienus; and Marcus Porcius Cato ('Cato the Younger') – embarked the remains of Pompey's army and sailed for northern Africa to join the king of Numidia, Juba I, who possessed a powerful army. Having dealt with Pharnaces, Caesar knew he would have to cross the Mediterranean Sea to confront them; but before he could do so, he had to travel to Rome, where some of his veteran legions, including his favourite *legio X*, had revolted. Caesar calmed the uprising with further promises of bounty and grants of land and set off for Africa.

While Caesar was occupied in Egypt, Asia and Italy, Pompey's generals consolidated their position in northern Africa and rebuilt their army. Scipio took overall command. As Caesar gathered his forces at Lilybaeum (modern-day Marsala, Sicily) in December 47 BC, he received reports that Scipio had amassed ten legions of Roman troops, and a large number of foreign cavalry. The legions were made up of men who had escaped from Pharsalus and reinforced with recruits from the Roman province of Africa. Many of these recruits were the descendants of Roman soldiers who had been granted land in Africa at the end of their service. So many farmers were levied that the crops that year remained standing in the fields, as there was no one left to harvest them (*BAfr.* 20). Others were drawn from classes of men normally ineligible for legionary service, including Africans, freedmen and slaves. The Pompeians were supported by Juba I, who had four legions of his own, presumably equipped and trained like Roman units, thousands of light cavalry who rode without saddles or bridles, substantial numbers of light infantry, bridled cavalry and more than 100 elephants (*BAfr.* 1).

By the third week of December, Caesar had assembled six legions and about 2,000 cavalry at Lilybaeum. Only one of the legions was a veteran unit, likely *legio V* (the *Alaudae*, raised in Gaul); the other five (XXV, XXVI, XXVIII, XXIX and one other, possibly XXX) were mostly composed of fresh recruits. Caesar embarked all the troops he could, and on 25 December sailed for Hadrumetum (modern-day Sousse), a town on the north-eastern coast of what is now Tunisia. During the short crossing, a storm scattered the fleet, so that when Caesar landed at Hadrumetum he had only 3,000 legionaries and 150 cavalry with him. The rest of the ships were spread around the coast. With such a small force of mostly raw recruits, Caesar could not take the town and decided to withdraw to a safe location to set up camp. As his men formed up into marching order, a group of Numidian horsemen attacked them, throwing javelins into the legionary ranks. Caesar's scanty cavalry fought them off, and the Numidians withdrew, only to attack the rear of the column again almost immediately. Caesar posted his few veteran cohorts as a rearguard, and between them and the cavalry they repulsed repeated assaults by the Numidians (*BAfr.* 6). This was Caesar's army's first experience of an entirely new style of fighting, to which they had to adapt quickly.

Over the next few days, Caesar was joined by the rest of his ships. He set up camp at a town called Ruspina (possibly modern-day Monastir, Tunisia) and sent messengers to his legates in Sicily with orders to embark more troops, and to Sardinia and other provinces to request further reinforcements, grain and supplies (*BAfr.* 8). Caesar's recruits were gripped with fear. They worried about the small size of their expeditionary force, their inexperience and the swarms of Numidian cavalry they had already encountered. Their only source of reassurance was the energy and confidence of their general (*BAfr.* 10).

Meanwhile, Labienus had been informed of Caesar's arrival and headed for Ruspina with a force of Numidian cavalry and light infantry. He hoped to destroy Caesar's small corps before reinforcements could arrive from Sicily. On the morning of 4 January 46 BC, the armies met on a flat, featureless plain near Caesar's camp. Labienus' Numidians nearly routed Caesar's recruits. Caesar only avoided disaster through his own decisive leadership, and because Labienus failed to press home his advantage. After safely withdrawing his army, Caesar reinforced his camp at Ruspina and waited for the rest of his troops to sail from Sicily. Fearing the arrival of Scipio and his enormous army, he disembarked the marines and archers from his ships and spread them around the camp. Caesar's men set up forges and started to manufacture weapons and cast lead bullets for sling shots. Caesar personally toured the walls of the camp every day, to check the defences and reassure his men (*BAfr.* 20–22). Scipio arrived, and joining his army with that of Labienus, set up a camp nearby. Their cavalry patrolled Caesar's camp and cut down any Caesarian soldiers who left the defences to collect water, food or fodder for their animals. To keep their horses from starving, Caesar's veterans fed them on seaweed collected from the beach. Caesar refused to accept battle until reinforcements arrived (Plutarch, *Vit. Caes.* 52).

After their ordeal at Ruspina, Caesar knew he needed to train his soldiers to deal with the Numidians' mode of fighting. He instigated a programme of basic infantry exercises, drilling his troops in all kinds of manoeuvres, to

A gold coin issued by Pharnaces II of Pontus. In early 47 BC, Pharnaces, the son of Mithridates VI Eupator whom Pompey had defeated 20 years earlier, invaded the north of Asia Minor (modern-day Turkey). Caesar's legate Gnaeus Domitius Calvinus confronted him with three legions, including some of Pompey's former soldiers who had surrendered after Pharsalus. Pharnaces defeated Domitius, and Caesar was forced to march to Pontus himself. Caesar met Pharnaces in battle at Zela (modern-day Zile, Turkey) on 2 August 47 BC with a small and hastily recruited army. Caesar's troops withstood a vicious attack by Pharnaces' scythed chariots, and after a brutal battle, routed him from the field. (Classical Numismatic Group, Inc. http://www.cngcoins.com/Wikimedia/CC BY-SA 2.5)

The famous Stoic Marcus Porcius Cato, known as 'Cato the Younger', was an enemy of Caesar's. He joined Scipio in Africa and took command of the city of Utica on the coast. After the battle of Thapsus, Cato took his own life, denying Caesar the opportunity to pardon him. Cicero wrote a widely circulated speech in praise of Cato. Caesar responded with his own work, entitled simply *Anticato*. (DEA/G. DAGLI ORTI/De Agostini via Getty Images)

improve their fighting skills, but also their confidence. The constant javelin attacks of the Numidian cavalry were a particular cause of anxiety (*BAfr.* 72). To improve his legions' flexibility, and their ability to counter the Numidian threat, Caesar ordered 300 men in each legion to march unburdened by their usual packs (*BAfr.* 75).

A few days later, Caesar's men were delighted to welcome a convoy of ships from Sicily, bringing the veteran *legio XIII* and *legio XIIII*, 1,000 archers and slingers and 800 Gallic horsemen. Another convoy arrived with grain shortly thereafter. Caesar now felt strong enough to take his army on the offensive against Scipio. He broke out of his camp at Ruspina and attempted to besiege the nearby town of Uzitta. At the same time, Juba arrived with his

Even some of the simplest Roman legionary helmets carried some sort of decoration around the rim, in this case a series of lines and a 'wave' design. Also visible is a hole pierced in the neck guard. The leather chinstrap was passed through this hole and down to the bottom of each cheek piece to hold the helmet firmly in place. A second strap may also have been strung through this hole to allow the helmet to be attached to a pack. (INTERFOTO/Alamy Stock Photo)

army from Numidia, bringing with him three of his own legions, 800 cavalry with bridles and a great number of Numidian horsemen (who rode without saddles or bridles) and light infantry, accompanied by elephants. He joined up with Scipio, whose legionaries were overjoyed by the size of their allies' force.

Caesar ordered his men to construct a fortified camp on a hill near Uzitta. From there, assisted by two more veteran legions recently arrived from Sicily, *legio IX* and *legio X*, they began to build a pair of walls that stretched up to the town. Caesar wanted to protect his flanks from cavalry attack when they assaulted Uzitta. The ramparts, however, also provided a safe route for Scipio's men to desert and many soldiers from Scipio's *legio IV* and *legio VI*, as well as African and foreign cavalry, took the opportunity to change sides (*BAfr.* 52). When the walls were complete, Caesar stationed a line of catapults at a safe distance and his men began a constant barrage into the town. Scipio built his own camp close by.

Early in the morning, Scipio led out his whole force, including the units belonging to Juba, and formed up near the town. Caesar marched his men from the camp to meet them, and the two sides assembled only a quarter of a Roman mile (about 370m) apart. Caesar rode around his legions, encouraged his men, and gave the signal to wait for Scipio's troops to advance. He thought that Scipio would be so confident in his superior numbers, and the speed and agility of his Numidians, that he would attack first. The two armies stood ready until late afternoon. The soldiers of both sides must have spent the day in terror, expecting any moment to engage in what would have been a cataclysmic battle. Before night fell, however, Caesar ordered his men to withdraw behind the walls of his camp. It is not clear why Scipio refused to fight.

1 On 4 April, Caesar marches for the port city of Thapsus. Arriving the same day, he begins construction of a crescent-shaped line of emplacements to cut off the city, and blocks access from the south with a fort manned by three cohorts.

2 Scipio arrives on 5 April. His scouts report the access north is blocked by Caesar's fort, so Scipio leaves several legionary cohorts and light infantry in two camps commanded by Juba and Afranius at the southern end of the marsh to prevent Caesar withdrawing in that direction.

3 Scipio leads the rest of his forces around the outside of the marsh. They march overnight and begin the construction of a camp to the north before dawn.

4 Caesar's scouts report the arrival of Scipio's army. Caesar sends half of the fleet around the coast with orders to moor up near the shore behind Scipio's camp, and marches to meet Scipio.

5 Scipio draws up his forces in front of his camp, with elephants arrayed in front of both wings. Caesar arrives and deploys his own army. He divides *legio V* into two and stations its troops behind the wings as a fourth line to counter Scipio's elephants.

6 Caesar's men observe the confused and ill-disciplined movements of Scipio's troops and attempt to advance, against Caesar's orders. Caesar relents and the assault begins. Caesar's missile troops unleash a ferocious barrage against the elephants.

7 The elephants panic and trample out of control through Scipio's lines. Scipio's Numidian cavalry turn and flee. Caesar's men outflank the elephants and take Scipio's camp.

8 Scipio's men rout and try to reach the camps of Juba and Afranius.

9 Scipio's troops first reach the camp held by Afranius, hoping to regroup there and make a stand against Caesar's pursuing forces, but the camp has been abandoned. The leaderless men move on to Juba's camp, only to find the Numidians have also fled. Caesar's soldiers arrive and begin a terrible slaughter.

Battlefield environment

Thapsus was situated on a promontory. North of the town, a slender islet curved away to the west. About 1½ Roman miles (roughly 2.25km) inland of Thapsus was the lake or marsh of Moknine. In wet weather during the winter months, the marsh filled with water and became a lake and dried to a marsh again in the heat of the summer. In April, the lake was likely full of water, forcing both armies to approach Thapsus along narrow strips of land beside the coast to the east and north of the lake. Despite being very close to the sea, there were several high points in the landscape which controlled these constricted routes. Caesar occupied and fortified one strategic point south of Thapsus, and a detachment of only three cohorts was able to prevent Scipio's army from approaching from that direction. Scipio had to divert around the western side of the lake.

The ground near the edge of the lake was likely to have been soft and wet, which would have hampered the movement of soldiers. More consequentially, it would have restricted the mobility of Scipio's Numidian cavalry, who, unable to make their lightning attacks and withdrawals, would have been rendered ineffective. In the event, they played little part in the battle.

A view over the marsh or lake of Moknine. (Patrick Chapuis/ Sygma via Getty Images)

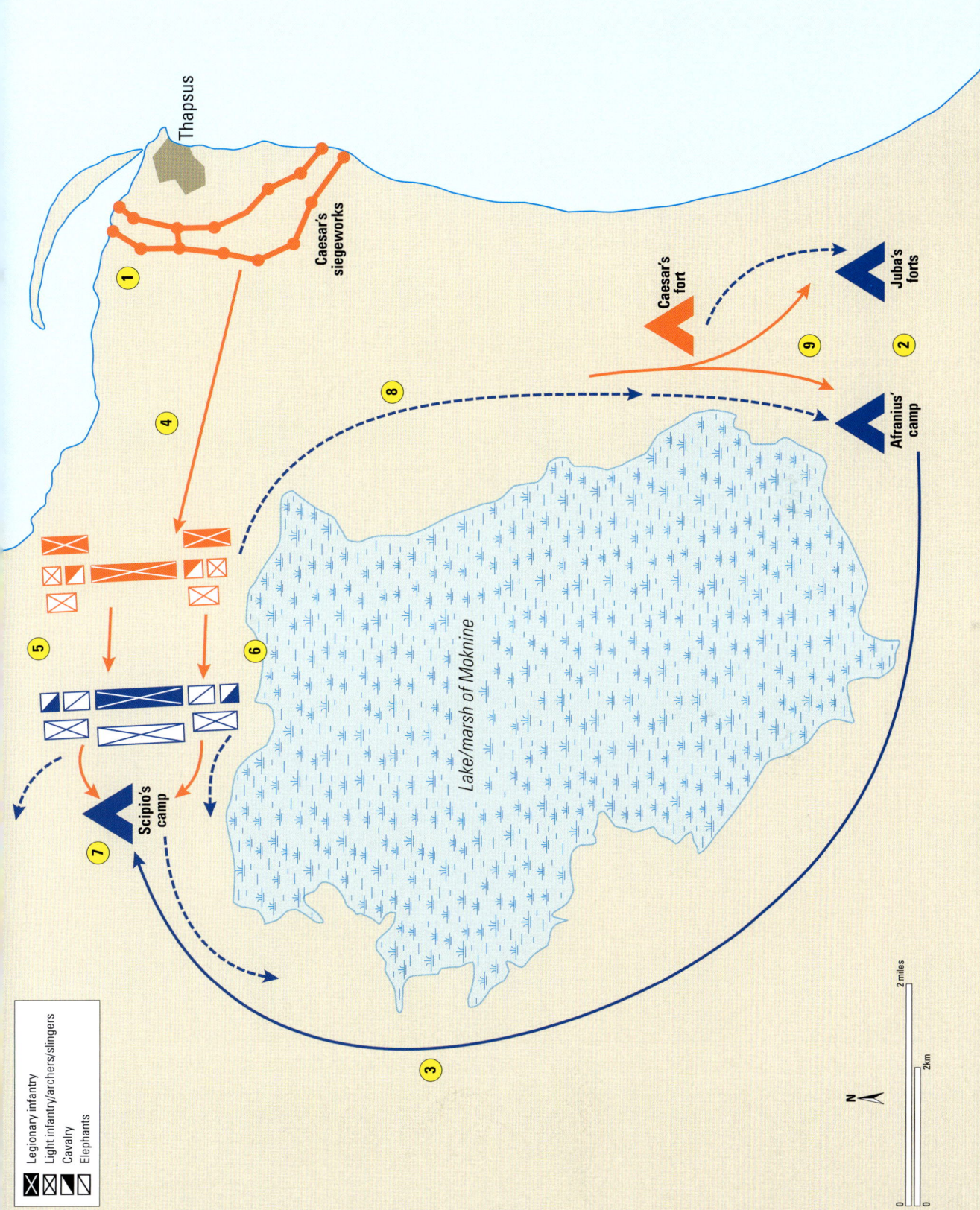

Thapsus

Caesar's siegeworks

Caesar's fort

Juba's forts

Afranius' camp

Scipio's camp

Lake/marsh of Moknine

1
2
3
4
5
6
7
8
9

Legionary infantry
Light infantry/archers/slingers
Cavalry
Elephants

N

2 miles
2km

INTO COMBAT

For the next few weeks, Caesar kept his army constantly on the move. He hoped that by advancing against towns holding significant supplies of grain, he would force Scipio to battle. Scipio continued to shadow Caesar's army but, though Labienus and the Numidian cavalry constantly harried Caesar's column, Scipio declined to engage his full force. At the beginning of April 46 BC, the last of Caesar's troops arrived from Sicily: a further 4,000 legionary reinforcements, 400 horsemen and 1,000 more archers and slingers. His army strengthened, Caesar marched for the coastal town of Thapsus (near modern-day Bekalta, Tunisia) on 4 April. The people of Thapsus were loyal supporters of Scipio, and the town was held by Scipio's legate Gaius Vergilius and a large garrison (*BAfr.* 79). As soon as Caesar's men reached the walls of the town, they began to construct a siege rampart, and occupied several high points nearby, which they fortified. Caesar stationed three cohorts of his legionaries in a fort that commanded the narrow access to Thapsus from the south, between the lake or marsh of Moknine, and the sea. The town of Thapsus was built on a promontory, and so Caesar's troops were able to seal it off on the landward side with a crescent-shaped line of entrenchments. He brought up his fleet to blockade Thapsus from the sea (*BAfr.* 79–80).

Scipio could not afford to lose the loyal community of Thapsus, nor its large garrison. He marched his army from the south, hoping to reach the town through the narrow approach between the marsh and the sea. He halted his army about 8 Roman miles (roughly 12km) from Thapsus and built two fortified camps. When his scouts reported that the route north was effectively blocked by Caesar's fort, Scipio decided not to waste time and men on an assault. Instead, he divided his forces. Juba and Lucius Afranius, Pompey's legate from Hispania, remained in the two camps with several legionary cohorts and light infantry to prevent Caesar's army from withdrawing in that direction, while Scipio led most of the combined Roman and Numidian force around the western side of the marsh. In this way, Scipio hoped to trap Caesar and annihilate his army.

Scipio's troops circumnavigated the marsh during the night, but the column must have made slow progress. It would have been difficult for such a large body of men to travel quietly across the wet, muddy terrain, particularly for those at the back of the column, trudging through mud after it had been churned up by thousands of men and horses, and perhaps 100 elephants. Just before dawn, Scipio's men heard the order to halt and begin the construction of a camp. They were only 1½ Roman miles (about 2.25km) from Caesar's crescent of fortifications around Thapsus. As soon as the growing light revealed the arrival of Scipio's army, Caesar's scouts reported to their general. Caesar acted immediately. He left two legions, probably two of his recently recruited units, behind to guard the siegeworks and ordered the rest of his legionaries to form up outside the camp without their packs. Caesar then sent messengers out to the fleet. Some of the ships were to remain stationed off Thapsus. The rest were to sail round behind Scipio's camp, and then approach as close as possible to the shore. There they were to stay and await further orders (*BAfr.* 80).

Scipio drew up most of his army in front of his unfinished camp. Several cohorts remained within, and hastily continued the construction work. The main source for the battle, the anonymous author of *De Bello Africo*, does not give a detailed disposition of Scipio's forces at Thapsus, but he does describe how Scipio's army was arrayed outside Uzitta a few weeks earlier (*BAfr.* 59), and it is reasonable to assume that the order of battle at Thapsus was similar. In the centre, Scipio placed his Roman, and Juba's African, legions. Behind these, in a long thin line, was a reserve of Numidian light infantry. To the right and left of the legions Scipio positioned elephants, evenly spaced, with light infantry between them. At Uzitta, there was no space for cavalry on the left wing, but in the open ground near Thapsus, Scipio probably placed his bridled cavalry, and his many thousands of Numidian light horsemen, beyond the elephants on both wings. From there the light horsemen could swing out from the line on each side and try to surround Caesar's forces.

Caesar assembled his army for battle in three lines. In the centre he likely placed his newly recruited legions. On the left and right wings, he stationed his veteran units. There is unfortunately some doubt about the *De Bello Africo* manuscript here, and it is not clear which of Caesar's legions were on each wing. Nevertheless, we do know that Caesar divided *legio V Alaudae* into two. He positioned five cohorts of this reliable unit behind each wing to form a fourth line where they were most needed – directly opposite the elephants. In front of the wings Caesar arrayed his archers and slingers, and to each side his Gallic and German cavalry interspersed with lightly armed troops. Caesar's men were delighted to see him hurrying around his battle line on foot, cheering on his soldiers. He warmly reminded his seasoned troops of their previous victories, and encouraged his recruits, who had not yet experienced pitched battle, to try to emulate the bravery of the veterans, and win for themselves the status and reputation that their more experienced comrades had already earned *(BAfr. 81)*.

As Caesar's legions stood ready, Scipio's army was already in disarray. The legionaries manning the rampart were beginning to panic. They had received no clear orders, and though Caesar's entire army was formed up outside, they did not know whether they were to remain behind their fortifications or march out of the camp. In the confusion, some centurions attempted to lead their soldiers through the gates, only to return in disorder. The lack of leadership and discipline in Scipio's army was obvious to Caesar's men, and his officers and veterans began to clamour for their general to order the assault. They exclaimed that the chaos in their enemies' ranks was a portent from the gods, foretelling their victory. Caesar refused to give in to their pleas and urged his centurions to restrain their men. Suddenly, from far out on the right wing, the blare of a trumpet echoed along the line, giving the signal to attack. Every cohort surged forward as one, despite the screams of their centurions, who attempted to block their advance. Caesar realized he stood no hope of preventing the assault. He leapt on his horse, shouting 'Good luck!', and charged to the head of his army *(BAfr. 82–83)*. Hearing the shouts and the bellow of trumpets, the sailors on Caesar's ships let out a great roar and clashed their weapons, causing Scipio's ill-prepared soldiers to turn in alarm, and lose focus on the approaching Caesarians.

Coin minted by Scipio (Quintus Caecilius Metellus Pius Scipio Nasica) in 47 or 46 BC, when he commanded the Pompeian army in northern Africa. The symbol of the elephant on the reverse is common on Roman coins related to Africa. The head on the obverse is an image of the Roman god Jupiter, but his hair and beard are portrayed in the style worn by Numidian kings such as Juba I (r. 60–46 BC) and his ancestors. (Classical Numismatic Group/Wikimedia/CC BY 2.5)

The troops of Scipio's left wing were the first to face the onslaught. Arrows, slingstones and lead bullets hailed down around them, smashing into the troops' helmets and piercing their raised shields. The main target of Caesar's missile troops was the elephants, which, despite the placations of their handlers, were utterly terrified by the whistling barrage of missiles. The great beasts spun around and started running madly in all directions, beyond the control of their handlers. The soldiers between the elephants gave up all thought of fighting, their only concern now being to keep out of the way of the rampaging animals. Many of the soldiers were trampled to death as the elephants tried to force their way back through Scipio's ranks to the gates of the rampart.

On Caesar's left wing, the soldiers of his *legio V* pressed on with their assault, and closed with the elephants there. One of the enraged animals, bleeding from several wounds, attacked an unarmed soldier, pinning him under its front feet before crushing the life out of him with its knees. A veteran of *legio V* rushed forward to help, his weapon raised. Abandoning the now dead soldier, the elephant stood up, grasped the legionary with its trunk, and lofted him into the air. With a frantic chopping of his sword, the legionary so injured the elephant's trunk that it dropped him, and fled, screaming, gurgling and spraying blood from its trunk, back through its own lines (*BAfr.* 84).

Both wings collapsed into pandemonium. Scipio's Numidian cavalry, seeing the havoc caused by the rioting elephants, routed, and most left the battlefield. Caesar's cohorts managed to get behind the frenzied mass of men and elephants, and occupied Scipio's camp with little resistance. Scipio's legionaries retreated in unruly mobs, hoping to reach what they thought would be the safety of the two camps held by Afranius and Juba that they had left the previous day. They reached Afranius' camp to find it forsaken by its commander. When they realized there were no officers present around whom they could rally, they fled on to Juba's camp nearby, only to find it already taken by Caesar's legions. The exhausted soldiers grouped together on a low hill and made a show of lowering their arms, hoping for mercy from Caesar's men. They received no such thing. Caesar's soldiers, crazed by the intensity of battle, slaughtered them. So frenzied was the killing that Caesar's legionaries even turned on their own officers and killed several (*BAfr.* 85).

When the massacre was over, Caesar assembled his officers. He had taken all three enemy camps and soundly defeated Scipio's army for the loss of only 50 of his own men, though many were wounded. Thousands of Scipio's

A clay statuette of an elephant carrying a turret and a handler, found at Pompeii, Italy. Juba's elephants were equipped with fighting towers, secured with thick chains. Scipio recognized the potency of elephants in battle, but also the risk they posed to his own troops if their handlers lost control. He instructed his men to train the elephants to remain steady in battle in the following way: he formed two lines of soldiers, one of slingers, acting as the enemy, and the other of his own legionaries, and drew up the elephants between them. The slingers pelted the elephants with small stones. When the animals turned to flee, Scipio's soldiers launched their own barrage of stones, turning the elephants back towards the enemy (*BAfr.* 27). Despite this careful and dangerous training, at the battle of Thapsus, Scipio's elephants proved unreliable. (DEA/L. PEDICINI/De Agostini via Getty Images)

Facing Scipio's elephants

Here on Caesar's left wing, men of a veteran cohort of *legio V Alaudae* have advanced from their position in the fourth line to confront Scipio's elephants. The furious animals have been driven into a frenzy by the storm of stones and lead bullets launched by Caesar's slingers. The elephant on the right has thrown off his handler and is charging straight for the ranks of *legio V*, ears outstretched and trunk flailing. Though a well-aimed *pilum* has neutralized the Numidian spearman in the turret, the screaming animal will not be stopped so easily. In the centre, another elephant has wrapped its trunk around a Caesarian soldier and has lifted him into the air. The stalwart old legionary had rushed to assist an unarmed soldier, whom the elephant had attacked, and was crushing under its knees. As soon as the veteran approached with his *gladius* raised, the elephant abandoned the pulverized corpse and turned on him instead. The veteran is now hacking at the enraged animal with

his *gladius*, while the handler and the spearman in the turret strive to despatch him before he wounds the elephant too badly. They know that they stand little chance if the elephant panics.

A Numidian chieftain leads a group of horsemen in from the left, throwing his light javelin straight at the front rank of the cohort. As soon as his men have launched their weapons, they will wheel away on their agile mounts, giving the legionaries only a few seconds to respond with their *pila*. Beyond the cavalry, another elephant is running amok among the Numidian infantry, trampling anyone unable to get out of its way. Despite the efforts of its handler to regain control, the infuriated animal is heading straight into a group of Numidian light troops advancing on *legio V* from the right. Now is the time for the 'Larks' to press home their assault and reach the rampart of Scipio's camp.

Roman and African troops lay dead. Caesar's legionaries managed to round up the surviving elephants and drew them up in front of the walls of Thapsus, along with the rest of the army, in the hope of intimidating Vergilius and his defenders into abandoning further resistance. Caesar then rewarded his soldiers with grants of money and decorated those men who had shown particular bravery. After receiving no response from Vergilius, Caesar left three

A silver coin issued by Julius Caesar in Africa, 47–46 BC, showing the mythical hero Aeneas carrying his father Anchises out of the burning ruins of Troy. In his right hand, Aeneas holds the *Palladium*, a statue of the goddess Pallas Athena that was supposed to guarantee the safety of the city. According to Roman myth, Aeneas brought the *Palladium* to Italy when he founded the settlement that eventually became Rome. Julius Caesar's family claimed descent from Aeneas. The Roman poet Virgil (Publius Vergilius Marro) wrote an epic poem about Aeneas' journey from Troy to Italy, called the *Aeneid*, partly in support of Caesar's heir, Augustus, the first Roman emperor. (Met Museum/Rogers Fund, 1908/ Public Domain)

legions at Thapsus to maintain the siege, and marched north for the town of Utica, which was held by Cato the Younger. Cato committed suicide before Caesar arrived at Utica. Scipio escaped Africa but died at sea when his fleet was attacked during the battle of Hippo Regius. Afranius was captured in Africa and subsequently killed along with several other of Scipio's officers. Juba died in a joint suicide with his friend Marcus Petreius. The surviving Pompeian generals regrouped in Hispania.

Numidian cavalrymen depicted in relief on Trajan's Column in Rome. The Numidian cavalry wore no armour, and rode their swift, agile horses without a bridle or bit. (DEA/A. DAGLI ORTI/ De Agostini via Getty Images)

Munda

17 March 45 BC

BACKGROUND TO BATTLE

Bronze head of the Numidian king Juba II (r. 30–25 BC), found in Morocco and now in the Musée de l'histoire et des civilisations de Rabat, Morocco. Juba II was only an infant when his father was defeated at Thapsus, and was brought to Rome by Caesar, where he was carried in the triumphal procession celebrating Caesar's victory in 46 BC. (Fine Art Images/Heritage Images/Getty Images)

Caesar returned to Rome in the summer of 46 BC. He celebrated four triumphs (*triumphi*; victory processions) in honour of his campaigns in Gaul and Egypt, and his defeats of the two foreign kings, Pharnaces II and Juba I. Caesar did not commemorate his mastery in the civil war with a triumph, however. His enemies had been Roman citizens, and their generals, not least Pompey himself, had been senators and magistrates, and as such still commanded respect and affection among the Roman people. Caesar held a series of lavish entertainments in the city, including chariot racing, gladiatorial combats and banquets, and distributed a cash gift to the poorer citizens, the *plebs* ('plebians'), of 100 *denarii* each (Appian, *BCiv.* 2.101; Plutarch, *Vit. Caes.* 55).

Caesar rewarded his soldiers for their loyalty and long service. He gave the legionaries 5,000 *denarii*, centurions 10,000 *denarii* and his military tribunes and cavalry commanders 20,000 *denarii* each (Appian, *BCiv.* 2.102). He also fulfilled his promise to honour his retiring veterans with grants of land in new colonies. Some soldiers remained in Africa and settled around what is now the Cap Bon peninsula in north-eastern Tunisia. Veterans from *legio VI* set up a colony at Arelate (modern-day Arles, France), and those from *legio X* moved to nearby Narbo (modern-day Narbonne, France). Colonies for the retiring *legio VII* and *legio VIII* were established near Capua in Italy, and there were likely many smaller veteran communities founded elsewhere (Keppie 1984: 111–12).

The celebrations held in Rome were tempered by sadness at the human cost of the civil war. A census held in the city found the population to be only half what it had been before the conflict began. Italy and the provinces perhaps paid an even greater price (Appian, *BCiv.* 2.102; Plutarch, *Vit. Caes.* 55); but as much as Caesar, his veterans, and the people of Rome might have wished the war was over, the remnants of the Pompeian forces were determined to carry on fighting. After Thapsus, the survivors of Scipio's army had fled to the province of Hispania Ulterior ('Further Spain'), where they had joined Pompey's two sons, Gnaeus Pompeius 'the Younger' and Sextus Pompeius.

Hispania Ulterior had been in turmoil since 49 BC. After defeating Pompey's legates, Caesar had appointed as governor Quintus Cassius Longinus. Cassius was a poor choice, however. His corrupt and unjust rule provoked hatred among the local people and the legions Caesar had placed under his command, one of which (the *vernacular* or 'home-grown' legion) was probably recruited from local, i.e. non-citizen Spanish men. During the uprising against his governorship, Cassius survived more than one assassination attempt, and in 48 BC two of his legions, including the 'home-grown', revolted. Conflict ensued between Cassius and the renegade legions, and the governor of the neighbouring province of Hispania Citerior ('Nearer Spain'), Marcus Aemilius Lepidus was forced to intervene. Early in 47 BC Cassius tried to flee with the money he had extorted, but was killed in a shipwreck at the mouth of the Ebro River. He was replaced by Gaius Trebonius, who had served Caesar as a legate during the conquest of Gaul (Richardson 1996: 112–14).

Ruins of the Roman *forum*, the political, judicial and religious centre of the city. According to Appian (*BCiv.* 2.92–94) after defeating Pharnaces II of Pontus, Caesar returned to Rome to find the city in chaos. Rioting and conflict between armed gangs had become so serious that Mark Antony, who Caesar had left in charge, had been forced to place the *forum* under armed guard. Three legions had occupied the *Campus Martius*, where the Roman Army had historically mustered. They were demanding discharge, the payment of bounties promised by Caesar after the battle of Pharsalus, and grants of land. Even Caesar's favourite unit, *legio X*, had joined the mutiny. Caesar climbed the speaker's platform, and addressed them, but as 'citizens' not as soldiers. He told them they were no longer needed, and he swore to pay them what he had promised after the rest of his army had triumphed against his enemies in Africa. Many of the soldiers clamoured to be allowed to remain in service, fearing they would miss out on their share of the profits from the upcoming campaign. Others felt ashamed to have abandoned their commander when he still faced so many enemies abroad. Caesar turned to leave but lingered at the foot of the platform. Eventually, he turned and announced that he would not punish any of the mutineers, even the ringleaders, and would retain all the legionaries except the men of *legio X*, whose disloyalty had been the most painful. He pledged to grant the men plots of land from his own and public land when all his enemies had been defeated. Caesar then set off for Africa. (DEA/M. Borchi/Getty Images)

According to the Greek historian Cassius Dio, the rebellious legions initially appeared to accept the leadership of Trebonius but, fearing retribution from Caesar, secretly sought support from Scipio in Africa. Scipio sent Gnaeus Pompeius to assist, with orders first to invade the Balearic Islands, and then to establish a base there from which he could launch an expedition to bolster the resistance to Caesar in Hispania Ulterior. Gnaeus successfully occupied the Balearics but was detained by illness, during which time Scipio and his generals were defeated at Thapsus. The Spanish renegades could not wait for Gnaeus, and incited communities across Hispania Ulterior to revolt. Trebonius was driven from the province. Gnaeus landed soon thereafter and, joined by the two rebellious legions, laid siege to the important coastal city of Carthago Nova ('New Carthage'; modern-day Cartagena, Spain), which had refused to join the uprising. During the summer of 46 BC, the surviving Pompeian generals, including Gnaeus' brother Sextus, Labienus and the former governor of Africa, Publius Attius Varus arrived, bringing with them the remains of Scipio's fleet and hundreds of soldiers (Cassius Dio, 43.29–31).

Caesar was preoccupied in Rome. He initially underestimated the scale of the insurrection in Hispania Ulterior and hoped his legates Quintus Fabius Maximus and Quintus Pedius would be able to defeat Gnaeus Pompeius with the legions already under their command (Cassius Dio, 43.31; *BHisp.* 2). Urgent reports soon reached Caesar in Rome, however, begging him to bring an army to Hispania to deal with the expanding threat. Caesar could not refuse. He left Rome in the hands of Lepidus, and marched for Hispania Ulterior, collecting some of his recently discharged veterans from their new colonies on the way. He reached the city of Corduba (modern-day Córdoba, Spain), which was under siege by Sextus Pompeius, in only 27 days, surprising both the enemy, and his own men, as he arrived before they even knew he was in Hispania (Cassius Dio, 43.32).

By the time Caesar arrived at Corduba, Gnaeus Pompeius had command of an army of 13 legions, cavalry and light infantry. According to the anonymous author of the *Bellum Hispaniense* (Spanish War), only four of the legions were reliable: the two that had rebelled against Cassius and then Trebonius (the 'home-bred' and probably *legio II*); a 'colonial' legion recruited from Roman citizens living in Hispania; and a legion of soldiers who had previously served under Afranius and had come to Hispania from Africa. The other legions were formed from slaves and local auxiliaries (*BHisp.* 7).

Caesar's army in Hispania was composed of eight legions. He brought with him four legions of veterans: *legio III*; *legio V Alaudae*, its men proudly displaying their new legionary emblem, the elephant, awarded by Caesar in recognition of their stalwart action against Scipio's elephants at Thapsus; the long-serving *legio VI*; and his favourite, *legio X*. The other four were newly recruited units, two of which may have been already stationed in Hispania under the legates Pedius and Fabius. The heavy infantry of the legions was supported by cavalry, some of whom arrived after Caesar, and many light troops.

1 On the morning of 17 March, Caesar's scouts inform him that Gnaeus Pompey 'the Younger' has drawn up his army for battle on the hillside below the fortified town of Munda. Caesar marches out into the plain below the town and deploys his own forces.

2 Caesar waits for Gnaeus to bring his army down onto the plain. When it is clear that Gnaeus is not going to descend, Caesar advances across the marshy ground and crosses the stream to close with Gnaeus' forces on the hillside.

3 Wary of his disadvantage at the foot of the hill, Caesar orders his troops to hold their positions. Gnaeus' troops assume the Caesarians are too afraid to advance and move a short way down the slope. The two sides engage.

4 After hours of fierce fighting, when both sides are evenly matched, Caesar's *legio X* mounts a determined assault on the right wing. Gnaeus' troops begin to give way, and he orders another of his legions to move across to reinforce the faltering line.

5 Caesar commands his cavalry to attack Gnaeus' line, thus preventing Gnaeus' legion from reaching the collapsing right wing.

6 Unable to resist *legio X*'s onslaught, Gnaeus' legionaries turn and flee for their camp. Caesar's men follow, break into the camp and cut down the troops sheltering there. Some of Gnaeus' men reach the safety of the fortifications around Munda.

Battlefield environment

The campaign in Hispania Ulterior was concentrated around the watershed of the Baetis (now the Guadalquivir) River and its tributaries, including the Salsum (now the Guadajoz) River. The terrain was mountainous, with high ranges separated by wide, fertile river valleys. Most of the local towns were built on the tops of hills, where the steep slopes provided natural defence, as well as clear visibility of the plain below. Even remote farms and villages were built on peaks, fortified and furnished with watch towers. It was impossible for columns of troops to move in the valleys without being spotted, and many communities were almost impervious to siege (*BHisp.* 7–8).

The precise location of the town of Munda is unknown. The author of the *Bellum Hispaniense*, who was probably a

centurion or cavalry commander in Caesar's army, provides a precise description of the battlefield, however. Gnaeus Pompeius' army was encamped next to the walls of the fortified town, which was situated on a steep hilltop, high above a plain. Gnaeus' camp was protected both by the existing walls of Munda, and the favourable terrain. Caesar had set up his own camp on another hill on the far side. Where the hillside levelled out below Gnaeus' camp there was a stream, and the ground to Caesar's side of the stream was marshy and covered in boggy pits. The plain beyond the stream, however, was open and flat, and ideal for cavalry manoeuvres, particularly in the calm sunny weather on the day of the battle (*BHisp.* 28–29).

A view over the valley of the Guadalquivir (known in Roman times as the Baetis) River in Andalucia, Spain. The broad floodplain was ideal for the unimpeded movement of troops, and well suited to cavalry action. (De Agostini/Getty Images)

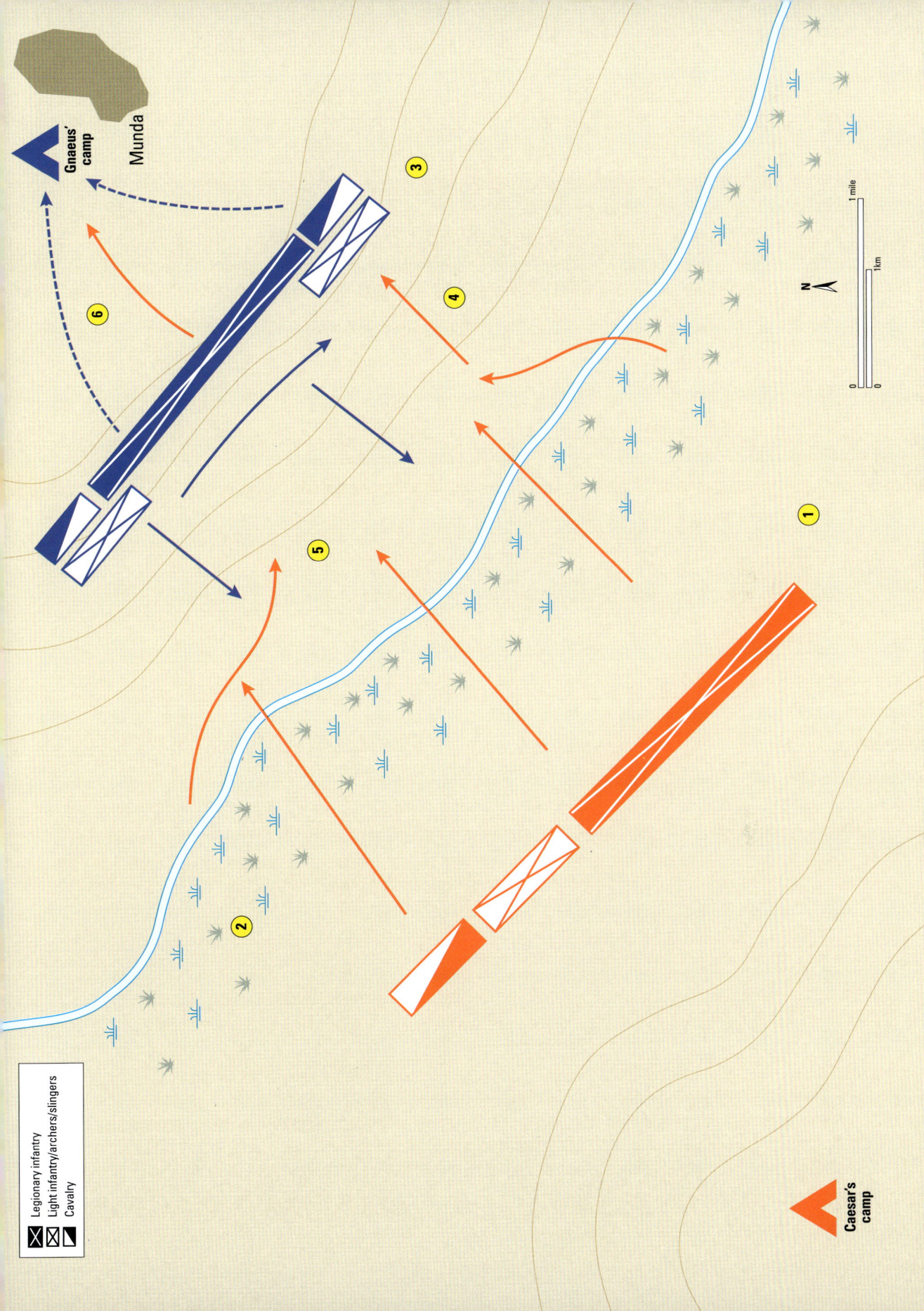

Munda

Gnaeus' camp

Caesar's camp

3

4

6

5

1

2

N

1 mile

1km

Legionary infantry
Light infantry/archers/slingers
Cavalry

INTO COMBAT

Caesar arrived in Hispania in the late autumn of 46 BC. He approached Corduba, on the banks of the Baetis (now the Guadalquivir) River, which was held by Sextus Pompeius and a large garrison. Gnaeus Pompeius and the main body of the Pompeian army were engaged in a siege of the nearby town of Ulia (modern-day Montemayor, Spain), one of the few communities in the area to oppose the insurrection. The people of Ulia managed to get a message to Caesar, pledging their allegiance. In response, Caesar sent a force of six cohorts of legionaries and an equal number of cavalry to assist the town, under the command of Lucius Vibius Paciaecius, who knew the area well (*BHisp.* 3).

At the same time, Caesar advanced on Corduba, hoping to force Gnaeus Pompeius to abandon his siege of Ulia and come to the aid of his brother. The bridge across the Baetis was controlled by Sextus Pompeius, so to reach the town, Caesar's men built their own crossing by dropping baskets full of stones into the water and laying wooden beams over the top. On the far side, they dug in next to the town in three camps. Gnaeus indeed arrived soon after and camped on the other side of the river. Caesar knew that to take Corduba, he would first have to take control of the permanent bridge and ordered his men to begin erecting a line of fortifications from his camp towards it. Gnaeus also understood that he could only protect the town by defending the bridge. For several days, the bridge was the focus of savage skirmishes, as both commanders tried to extend their fortifications up to the crossing; but despite bodies piling up on the riverbanks, neither side gained control. Caesar decided to withdraw from the town and moved out into the open plain that stretched either side of the river. He hoped that Gnaeus would follow him and engage his full force in open battle (*BHisp.* 5).

This was exactly what Gnaeus Pompeius did not want. Like his father, Pompey the Great, after Dyrrachium, and Scipio in Africa, Gnaeus wanted to avoid meeting Caesar in battle. Instead, he intended to wear Caesar's men down by keeping them on the move, preventing their access to food and fodder and constantly harassing them with small-scale attacks. Most of the communities in the Baetis valley supported the Pompeian cause and were thus hostile to Caesar. As the fighting dragged on into winter, conditions for both sides became increasingly harsh. The Pompeian legionaries, most of whom were inhabitants of the area, could shelter inside towns and villages, where there were plentiful supplies. Caesar's soldiers, however, had to sleep in tents and survive on what meagre rations they had brought with them or could forage locally (Cassius Dio, 32–33).

Caesar decided to assault a town called Ategua, on the Salsum (now the Guadajoz) River, about 20 Roman miles (roughly 30km) from Corduba, which held a significant store of grain. His legionaries built a ring of entrenchments around Ategua and constructed siege engines. To protect the siegeworks from a Pompeian counter-attack, they also occupied and fortified several nearby hills (*BHisp.* 7). Gnaeus Pompeius followed and set up his own camp on the other side of the river. The siege continued for weeks, as Caesar's men kept up almost daily assaults on the town, while Gnaeus' troops attacked their fortifications from behind, and prevented any attempt by the Caesarians to leave their entrenchments to gather supplies.

Ategua eventually surrendered on 19 February 45 BC. The fighting there was brutal, and atrocities were carried out by both sides. The author of the *Bellum Hispaniense* records one particularly heinous incident, in which Gnaeus' men dragged several hostages from among the townsfolk onto the walls and slit their throats in full view of Caesar's legionaries, before throwing their bodies off the wall (*BHisp.* 15). After the fall of Ategua, Gnaeus moved his forces to Ucubi (modern-day Espejo, Spain), a town situated a few kilometres to the south. Gnaeus' soldiers forced the inhabitants to assemble outside the gates and demanded to know who among them supported Caesar: 74 admitted their allegiance and were beheaded (*BHisp.* 20). The previous night, Caesar's men captured four scouts from the 'home-grown' legion, three of whom were slaves. They crucified the slaves and beheaded the fourth (*BHisp.* 20). Despite the merciless treatment that captives received, many Pompeian soldiers deserted to Caesar, including a military tribune and a standard bearer.

On 16 March, Caesar moved his army into a wide plain beneath the hilltop town of Munda. Gnaeus' legionaries had built a camp close to the walls of the town, in such a way that it was well protected by both the existing fortifications, and its lofty position. Caesar had his men construct their own marching camp on a hill on the far side of the plain, which was about 5 Roman miles (roughly 7.5km) wide. Early the next morning, Caesar was about to order his men to move on, when scouts arrived at his tent with news that in the early hours of the morning Gnaeus had formed up his entire army in battle formation. Caesar acted at once. He raised the signal flag to prepare for battle.

The *Bellum Hispaniense* (28–31) provides the best account of the encounter. Gnaeus had formed his 13 legions up in front of the combined defences of his camp and the walls of Munda, likely in the usual *triplex acies* or 'triple line' formation usually employed by the Roman Army. On each wing he stationed his cavalry, and in front of the whole array, a screen of 6,000 lightly armed troops and an equal number of auxiliaries. He kept his force close to the fortifications, where they had the advantage of height over Caesar's advancing army. They were also protected by a stream that ran through an area of marshy ground on the edge of the plain, close to the bottom of the slope.

As Caesar's army marched across the plain the weather was sunny and calm. Like Gnaeus Pompeius, Caesar had formed up his eight legions in three lines. The staunch veterans of *legio X* took up their usual position in the front rank of the right wing, while *legio III* and *legio V Alaudae* formed the

Coin minted by Quintus Cassius Longinus. Longinus was the brother (or perhaps cousin) of Gaius Cassius Longinus, one of the leaders of the conspiracy to assassinate Caesar. Quintus Cassius Longinus' unjust and avaricious governorship of the province of Hispania Ulterior turned the army against him, and fuelled anti-Caesarian sentiment among the people, both indigenous Spaniards and Roman colonists. It is not surprising that so many communities supported the sons of Pompey when they arrived in Hispania. (Johny SYSEL/Wikimedia/CC BY-SA 3.0)

mainstay of the left. Caesar placed the less experienced legions in the centre of the line, and placed his 8,000 cavalry, as well as his light infantry and auxiliaries, beyond the legions on the left flank. As his army advanced, Caesar and his men expected Gnaeus Pompeius' forces to descend from their elevated position close to the town walls to meet them in battle on the open plain. The Caesarian soldiers were delighted that they would be able to engage the enemy under such favourable conditions, particularly the cavalry, for whom the terrain was ideal. Some of the Caesar's men, however, were worried that, after all they had endured, the outcome of the whole war rested on what would happen in the next hour.

Even as the Caesarians approached the swampy ground at the foot of the hill, Gnaeus Pompeius' troops remained in their defensive lines next to the town and camp. Caesar was immediately concerned that, in their eagerness, some of his cohorts might break out from the line. He recalled what had happened at Thapsus, and feared that with Gnaeus' defensive advantage, the consequences of an undisciplined charge would be very different here. He ordered his men to hold their positions, and not advance beyond a certain point. When Caesar's men heard this, many were angry, as they felt that their commander was delaying them needlessly and hindering their chances of victory. The Pompeians on the hillside assumed their opponents were simply too frightened to engage, and confidently began to descend. As the two sides came within range, trumpets blared out across the plain. The gap closed to about 25m; the legionaries launched their heavy javelins with a deafening shout, drew their short swords, and charged.

The fighting was ferocious. Both sides maintained a furious tempo of javelin volleys, and as cohort smashed into cohort, the armies seemed closely matched. The Caesarian legionaries threw themselves uphill into the mêlée, but many started to worry that despite their courage, and their faith in their general, they could not overcome their enemy from so far below. The clamour of battle was too much for some of the inexperienced Caesarian soldiers: unable to escape the screams and moans of the wounded and dying, and the clanging of weapons, they were almost frozen by fear. According to Plutarch (*Vit. Caes.* 56) and Appian (*BCiv.* 2.104), Caesar himself began to despair that his legions were making no headway. He ran around his men, exhorting them to keep pushing up the hill. Caesar's flagging legionaries watched in astonishment as their commander removed his helmet, grabbed a shield from one of their comrades and sprinted towards the Pompeian line, screaming at them to follow. The Pompeians responded with a hurl of javelins, most of which missed, but Caesar had to deflect at least one with the shield. Caesar's officers ran to protect him. Shamed into returning to the fight, the Caesarian legionaries raced to join them.

The battle continued nearly all day, and for many hours neither side appeared to be overcoming the other. By late afternoon, hundreds of men on both sides had been killed and thousands wounded. In one last push, the veterans of Caesar's *legio X* rushed forward on the right wing, launching their heavy javelins before clashing into the Pompeian lines, shoving with their heavy shields and jabbing their short swords at bellies and faces. The exhausted Pompeians were unprepared for *legio X*'s relentless onslaught so late in the battle and began to give way. Gnaeus Pompeius immediately ordered

one of his legions to move across to reinforce their retreating comrades, thus temporarily weakening his line. Caesar's cavalry swept forward from the left and attacked the Pompeians so vigorously that their reinforcements could not reach their faltering left wing. The remorseless assault of *legio X* was too much. The Pompeian left wing collapsed into a rout, as Gnaeus' legionaries abandoned the line and fled for the safety of their camp and the fortified town of Munda. Caesar's legions surged up the hill in pursuit. Most of

Helmets of the Boeotian type were popular with Roman cavalry in the Republican period. Inspired by the soft felt hats worn by Greek horsemen, they were beaten into the correct shape from a single sheet of copper alloy. (Heritage Images/Hulton Archive/Getty Images)

the Pompeians made it through the gates of the camp but the Caesarians surrounded it and soon broke through the entrenchments. Once inside, they slaughtered the Pompeian defenders. Only the most fortunate reached the walls of the town.

The battle of Munda was the last major action of Caesar's civil war. In the following days, he remarked that though he had often had to struggle for victory, this was the first time he had ever had to fight for his own life (Plutarch, *Vit. Caes.* 56; Appian, *BCiv.* 2.104). He had lost over 1,000 of his own men, both infantry and cavalry, and over 500 wounded. The Pompeian dead exceeded 30,000, including Labienus and Varus. Gnaeus Pompeius was severely wounded, but survived the battle. The number of bodies was so great that Caesar ordered his men to pile them up into a rampart around the walls of Munda, with shields and javelins arranged into a palisade. On top of the heaped corpses, they impaled rows of severed heads onto sword points to intimidate the survivors into surrendering the town (*BHisp.* 32).

Caesar left a detachment of his army under Fabius to continue the siege, and they took the town several days later: 14,000 Pompeians were captured alive. Caesar marched for Corduba, hoping to catch Sextus Pompeius. Corduba had been occupied by three legions of refugees from Munda

This relief statue from Estepa, Spain, now in the Museo arquéologico de Córdoba, Spain, may show the appearance of soldiers in the local legions serving in Hispania during Caesar's civil war. The shields are unusual: though the long 'barleycorn' reinforcing spine and the boss are like those visible on other contemporary examples, the trapezoidal shape is almost unique. This may suggest they were adapted from local styles. The figure on the left appears to wear a coat of ring mail, while the figure on the right wears some kind of fabric body protection, perhaps made of thick quilt, worn over a reinforced undergarment that rises high up the neck and which may have been made from stiffened leather. Both soldiers also wear greaves and metal helmets of different styles. (Album/Alamy Stock Photo)

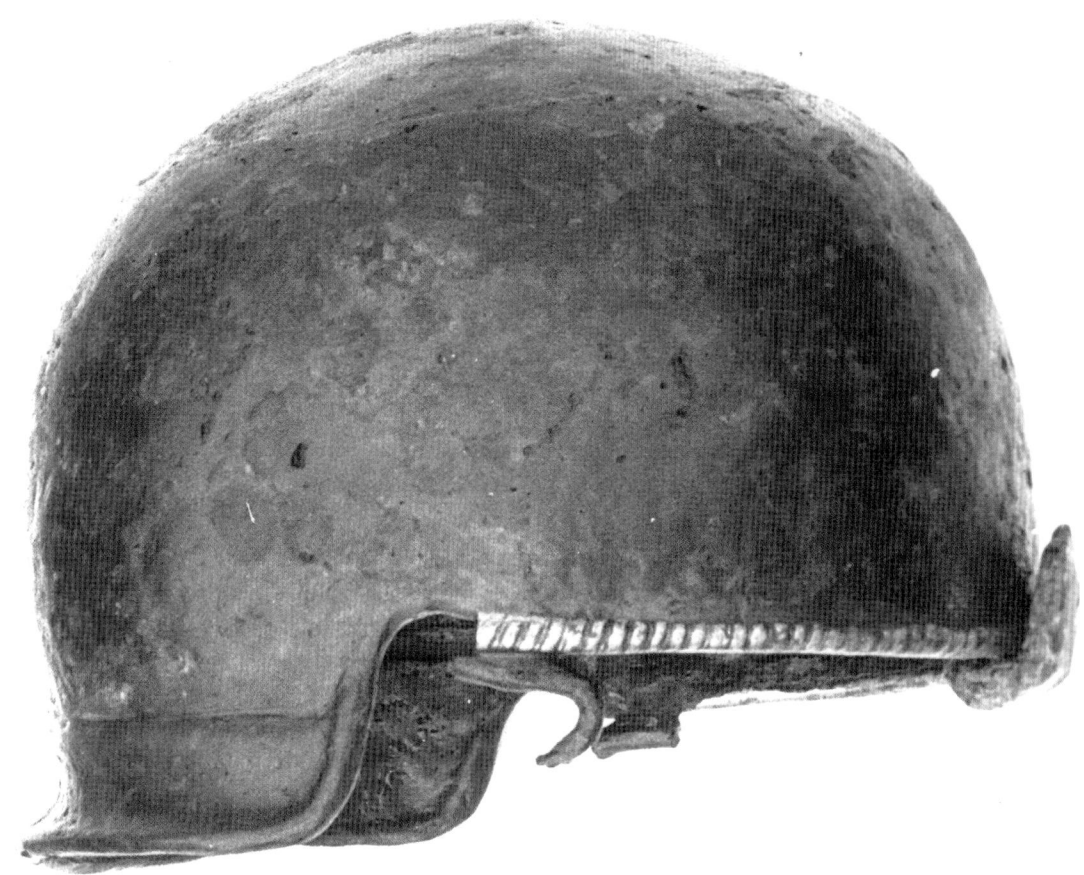

A helmet with a decorated headband, now in the Musée de Saint-Raymond in Toulouse, France. The slight indentation above the ears and the subtle flare at the neck are like the helmet worn by one of the figures on the Estepa relief from Spain. (Laboratoire d'Archéologie des métaux de Jarville/Musée Saint-Raymond/Wikimedia/Licence Ouverte 1.0)

and slaves whom Sextus had freed and armed. The Pompeians, however, disagreed about whether to resist or surrender to Caesar, and as fighting erupted between them, Caesar's men broke through the gates. They cut down the defenders, killing 22,000 of them (*BHisp.* 32–34). In this way, Caesar proceeded from town to town, seeking to regain control of the whole of Hispania Ulterior.

Gnaeus Pompeius and a few supporters escaped to the seaport of Carteia (close to modern-day Gibraltar). While the inhabitants argued about whether to give him sanctuary or surrender him to Caesar, Gnaeus and his men chose to flee in a fleet of 20 ships. In their haste, however, they left Carteia without food and water, and after only four days had to land to take on supplies. A squadron of ships commanded by one of Caesar's officers, Gaius Didius, caught up with them and set fire to several of their ships. Despite his wounds, and a sprained ankle, Gnaeus managed to scramble up into some nearby hills, where he hid in a rocky outcrop. Didius and a small force of infantry and cavalry soon surrounded his position and found him huddled in a cave in a ravine. They dragged Gnaeus from his hiding place, executed him, and delivered Caesar his severed head. Gnaeus' brother Sextus remained elusive. He continued to lead the resistance to Caesar in Hispania Ulterior, and by the following year was in command of a force of six legions and had recaptured several towns.

Analysis

DYRRACHIUM

The fighting at Dyrrachium can be divided into three phases. The first was the 'construction phase', when the two armies raced to build competing lines of fortifications around the hill at Petra. This was followed by the second, 'static phase', in which Pompey's legions and allied missile troops mounted a series of raids on Caesar's forts, and Caesar's men tried to maintain their blockade of the Pompeian army. The third and final 'mobile phase', which lasted only one day, ensued when Pompey discovered from the Gallic traitors that Caesar's fortifications were incomplete.

Caesar's legions were far more experienced in construction work than their Pompeian counterparts. During the conquest of Gaul, they had operated for long periods in hostile territory, which required the fast and efficient erection of fortified camps on an almost daily basis. Caesar's legions had also constructed several enormous complexes of fortifications, such as the double-circumvallation with which they surrounded Alesia in Gaul in 52 BC. At Dyrrachium, despite having significantly fewer men, Caesar's soldiers built a line of forts and entrenchments over 17 Roman miles (about 25.5km) long, which enveloped Pompey's army. Had Caesar's men had more time, they would likely have completed the seaward section of the walls at the southern extent, completely blockading the Pompeians, who, trapped in the increasingly insanitary conditions within the cordon and unable to feed their starving horses, may have had to withdraw by sea.

Though the Caesarians had the advantage in the 'construction phase', Pompey's soldiers were better equipped to engage in the 'static phase' that followed. The large contingent of allied missile troops that accompanied the legionaries in their regular assaults forced their opponents to remain within their defences and endure horrific bombardments, such as that inflicted on Scaeva's fort. Caesar's men had only stones with which to

After a battle, victorious Roman generals often displayed the armour and weapons of their enemies as 'trophies'. This example, carved in relief on the San Omobono monument base displayed in the Museo Centrale Montemartini in Rome, features helmets with transverse crests, indicating a command role. The ornate cuirass on the left was a type of armour worn by Roman officers, such as military tribunes and legates, and their rank was denoted by the sash tied around the waist. The *pteryges* provided some protection to the groin and upper legs, while allowing freedom of movement, including riding a horse. (Stefano Ravera/Alamy Stock Photo)

respond. While less experienced and determined troops than Caesar's would not have maintained such a steadfast grip on their positions under such onslaughts, even Caesar's veterans could not have resisted many more coordinated Pompeian attacks on multiple strongpoints. Both sides faced terrible conditions at Dyrrachium, though Caesar's men perhaps suffered the most due to their lack of food and other supplies, which their Pompeian opponents could receive by ship.

The 'static phase' was ended, not through attrition but treachery. The Allobroges brothers' vital intelligence provided the means to penetrate the blockade and initiated the brief 'mobile phase' of the battle. Pompey's dawn assault on the incomplete section of Caesar's fortifications exposed a surprising weakness in the Caesarian legionaries' resolve, considering (or perhaps because of) all they had endured. The confused and chaotic withdrawal of *legio IX*, and the cowardly failure of their reinforcements, allowed the Pompeians to inflict many casualties, and foreshadowed the humiliating rout of Caesar's legions from *legio IX*'s former fort later that day. As Caesar himself noted (*BCiv.* 3.72), due to the confined space, and the large numbers of men that had charged inside, when his legionaries tried to escape through the narrow gates of the fort, they caused more damage to themselves than they sustained from Pompey's soldiers – but Pompey failed to press home the attack. It is hard not to agree with Caesar that the Pompeians could have ended the war that day, had they been led by a general who knew how to win (Appian, *BCiv.* 2.62).

THAPSUS

By the time Caesar assembled his expeditionary force at Lilybaeum in December 47 BC, he was in control of most of the Roman Empire. The resources of manpower, *matériel* and money at his disposal were enormous. Yet Caesar was presented with the same challenge that all generals face when preparing for a seaborne invasion of hostile territory: though they may be in possession of greater martial resources than their enemy, they still face the difficulty of getting them onto shore and establishing a secure beachhead into which the rest of the army and *matériel* can be poured. In his haste, Caesar did not wait until his whole army had massed at Lilybaeum and embarked only a small force of mostly inexperienced recruits. These men arrived in Africa with little training and were terrified by the hordes of indigenous soldiers they immediately encountered. The poor performance of Caesar's raw troops against the Numidian cavalry and light infantry at Ruspina shows how important proper training and battle experience was to the effectiveness of Roman legionaries during the civil war. Despite putting his recruits through a rigorous programme of basic training, it was not until his veteran legions arrived that Caesar felt sufficiently confident to attempt to engage Scipio's army in open battle.

Nearly all the fighting leading up to the battle of Thapsus was between Caesar's legionaries and Numidian cavalry and light infantry. Labienus boasted that he commanded so many of these troops that Caesar's men would be exhausted just with killing (*BAfr.* 19), and Caesar worried that his men were having so much difficulty dealing with the Numidians' coordinated attacks that they would not survive an encounter with the heavy infantry of the Pompeian legions as well (*BAfr.* 72). Yet Caesar needn't have worried. At Thapsus, the difference between the Caesarian and Pompeian legionaries was clear. The Pompeian legions proved to be poorly led, ill-disciplined and lacking in confidence. Their shambolic preparations for battle at the unfinished rampart of Scipio's camp gave Caesar's men such assurance of victory that they charged into battle against his orders. While Caesar worried about the overconfidence of his men, the Pompeians demonstrated a complete lack of faith in their commanders and themselves.

Yet Thapsus was ultimately decided by the failure of Juba's unpredictable and unreliable elephants to withstand the barrage of stones and lead bullets launched by Caesar's slingers. The havoc that followed the elephant handlers' loss of control tempted the Numidian cavalry to abandon the wings and gave Caesar's legions the opportunity to circle around the chaos and capture Scipio's camp, precipitating the wider rout. Caesar understood the danger the elephants posed, and the fear they instilled in his men. In the weeks preceding the battle of Thapsus, he had several elephants sent over from Italy, so that his soldiers could examine them and learn where they were vulnerable, especially when protected by armour. He also ensured his cavalry horses were introduced to the elephants so that they would not be alarmed by their unfamiliar appearance, trumpeting or scent (*BAfr.* 72). When faced with the great animals in combat, the soldiers of *legio V* tackled them with assurance. As in so many previous battles, elephants proved to be of dubious value.

Coin minted by Marcus Junius Brutus, one of the leaders of the conspiracy against Julius Caesar. In 54 BC Brutus was appointed to the post of *triumvir monetalis*, one of three men tasked with minting coins in the Roman Republic. It was common for those holding this office to commission the production of coins that celebrated the achievements of their ancestors. In a strange foreshadowing of his own role as a 'liberator' of the Republic from the autocratic rule of Caesar, on this coin Brutus chose to commemorate his ancestor Lucius Junius Brutus, who led the plot to expel the last Roman king, Lucius Tarquinius Superbus. Lucius Junius Brutus served as one of the Republic's first consuls, and he is depicted on the reverse in procession with his attendants, known as *lictores*. A female personification of 'liberty' is portrayed on the obverse. (Hulton Archive/Heritage Images via Getty Images)

MUNDA

The battle of Munda was the most closely fought of the civil war, and the one that Caesar himself felt he was nearest to losing. In complete contrast to Thapsus, at Munda the Pompeian legionaries proved themselves to be determined, effective soldiers, as they had from the beginning of the campaign. To understand why they were so impressive, it is necessary to consider their origins, experience and motivation.

The Pompeian legions were drawn from various backgrounds. Of the four legions that the anonymous author of the *Bellum Hispaniense* considered reliable, one was recruited from men who had previously served under Lucius Afranius, Pompey the Great's former legate in Hispania. After Afranius and his colleagues capitulated in 49 BC, Caesar disbanded their legions and discharged the soldiers. Many of these subsequently re-joined the Pompeian army, travelling to Africa with their former commanders to fight under Scipio. Some were recruited, willingly or otherwise, into the legions that revolted from Cassius Longinus and then Trebonius. Others remained and joined up when Gnaeus Pompeius arrived in Hispania Ulterior. These experienced veterans formed the backbone of Gnaeus' army and fought with the strongest motivation: they knew that if defeated, they would not be released by Caesar a second time. These were, as Cassius Dio points out (43.36), desperate men whose only hope of safety lay in victory.

Two of Gnaeus Pompeius' legions were formed from local soldiers. The 'home-grown' legion was most likely recruited from Spaniards, who did not enjoy the benefits of Roman citizenship, and, though the soldiers of the 'colonial' legion probably were citizens, they were drawn from Roman communities founded in Hispania since the end of the Second Punic War in 201 BC. The families of these men could have been living in Hispania for generations. It is plausible that the soldiers of the two 'local' legions were motivated by a desire to resist or limit external Roman rule, particularly after the cruel governorship of Cassius Longinus. That so many communities continued to resist Caesar's attempt to regain control of the province after the battle, and that Sextus Pompeius was able to recruit his six legions of soldiers so quickly after Caesar left, suggest that anti-Roman feeling was, and remained, strong in Hispania. As for the rest of the army, the Spanish 'auxiliaries' probably shared the same anti-colonial aspirations, and unless Caesar could be defeated, the best the freed slaves could expect was a return to servitude. Finally, all those who had been involved in the legionary revolt knew they faced the severest punishment if defeated and captured. It is no surprise the Pompeian legionaries fought so tenaciously at Munda: they were fighting for their very lives.

Aftermath

Caesar returned to Rome in the autumn of 45 BC having won the civil war and achieved complete control of Rome and its provinces. He was made *dictator* for life, and elected consul, and set about reorganizing Rome and the Roman Empire with the same energy and efficiency with which he had commanded his armies. He again discharged his veterans, releasing those who had been recalled for the Munda campaign back to their colonies, and arranged for the establishment of many more such settlements.

Caesar did not intend to remain in Rome for long, however. By the beginning of March 44 BC, he had assembled a considerable army in preparation for a long campaign in the East against the Parthians, from whom he hoped to regain the legionary eagles lost by Marcus Licinius Crassus at Carrhae in 53 BC. This force included several of the legions he had recruited during the civil war, and some former Pompeian legions that had remained in the eastern provinces after Pharsalus. The *Alaudae* were also still in service, and they may have been intended for this campaign – but many senators

Coin issued by Octavian in 38 BC. Octavian is shown on the obverse (left) along with the inscription 'CAESAR DIVI F[ILIUS]' (Caesar, son of a god). On the reverse is a portrait of Julius Caesar, accompanied by the inscription 'DIVOS [IULIUS]' (Divine Julius). Julius Caesar was deified (declared a god) by the senate in 42 BC, after which Octavian, Caesar's adopted son and heir, styled himself as the son of a god. (Heritage Art/Heritage Images via Getty Images)

feared Caesar's power and decided to act while he was still in the city. Three days before he hoped to leave for Parthia, on the Ides of March (15 March), Caesar was stabbed to death at a senate meeting. He fell, bleeding from wounds from many knives, at the feet of a statue of Pompey.

Caesar's death shocked Rome. Mark Antony, Caesar's closest supporter and fellow consul, managed to calm the city, and the leaders of the conspiracy, Marcus Junius Brutus and Gaius Cassius Longinus, were allowed to leave and take up posts in the eastern provinces. Caesar was given a monumental funeral, and when his will was read out, it confirmed that he had nominated his sister's 19-year-old grandson, Gaius Octavius, as his heir. The young officer, who was in Macedonia helping to organize Caesar's army, changed his name to Gaius Julius Caesar Octavianus (from which his common English name 'Octavian' is derived), and headed straight for Rome.

Octavian was determined to claim his inheritance, at whatever cost. He recruited a small force, including veterans of Caesar's former *legio VII* and *legio VIII*, and confronted Mark Antony, whose legions included *legio V Alaudae*. After a conciliation, the two formed a 'Second Triumvirate' with Lepidus, who had persuaded the veterans of *legio VI* and *legio X* to leave retirement yet again. Octavian and Mark Antony then marched against Brutus and Cassius and defeated them at the battle of Philippi (on the coast of northern Greece) in 42 BC. For the following decade, Octavian and Mark Antony maintained an uneasy peace and divided the Roman Empire: Octavian took control of the west, and Mark Antony the east. War erupted between them in 32 BC. Octavian's victory in a naval battle in the seas off Actium in western Greece in the following year won him sole control of the Roman world.

In the civil wars that followed Caesar's assassination, most of his former legions were re-formed, and all ultimately ended up under the control of Octavian. Though the individual soldiers, many of whom had served for many years beyond the six normally expected for legionary service, were discharged, the units were retained. As Octavian transformed himself into 'Augustus', the first Roman emperor, he reorganized the Roman Army into a permanent, professional force. Caesar's stalwarts, including his favourite, *legio X*, and the feather-wearing *legio V Alaudae*, went on to serve the Roman emperors for decades.

The life-size head of a relief believed to depict the young Octavian, later Augustus, the first Roman emperor. During his reign, Augustus chose to portray himself in his portraits with youthful, idealized features. This was a clear break with the 'veristic' artistic tradition of the Roman Republic, in which elite men were shown as they appeared in life, usually in late middle age, with receding hairlines, pronounced wrinkles, a serious expression and penetrating gaze. (Sepia Times/Universal Images Group via Getty Images)

BIBLIOGRAPHY

Sources

The historian **Appian** (*c.*AD 95–*c.*165) was a member of a wealthy Greek family from Alexandria in Egypt. He held the office of *procurator*, a senior Roman official in the province, and worked as a legal advocate in Rome. In his later years, he wrote a history of Rome, focusing on the Roman Empire's many wars. Appian wrote in Greek, which was the dominant language used in the eastern Mediterranean in this period. His *Romaica* (Roman History) was divided into 24 books, only some of which survive. Five of the extant books concern the civil wars of the Late Republic. Book 2 covers the period of Caesar's civil war of 49–45 BC.

As well as being a gifted statesman, politician and general, **Gaius Julius Caesar** (*c.*100–44 BC) was a talented writer. *De Bello Civili* (The Civil War), his own commentaries on his civil war against Pompey the Great (106–48 BC), provide the most complete literary source for the first stage of the conflict. Written in clear, concise 'soldier's Latin', they cover the war in detail from its outbreak in 49 BC to the start of the Alexandrian War at the end of the following year. Accounts of the subsequent campaigns, *De Bello Alexandrino* (The Alexandrian War), *De Bello Africo* (The African War) and *Bellum Hispaniense* (The Spanish War), written by other writers whose identities are unknown, were collected with Caesar's in antiquity. The very different style of each of these three works suggests three separate authors, all of whom were, like Caesar, probably eyewitnesses to most of the events described. Caesar's commentaries on his conquest of Gaul, *Commentarii de Bello Gallico*, also survives. Unfortunately, his other literary works, including a long poem entitled *Iter* (The Journey), which he wrote in 24 days while travelling from Rome to Hispania Ulterior to confront Gnaeus Pompeius 'the Younger' in 46 BC, have been lost.

Marcus Tullius Cicero (106–43 BC) was the most influential orator and author of the Late Republic. Born into a wealthy family in Arpinum (modern-day Arpino), south-east of Rome, he entered public life as a lawyer and later pursued a political career. He was elected consul in 63 BC. During Caesar's civil war, Cicero sided with Pompey but returned to Rome after Pompey was defeated at Pharsalus. Cicero was not one of the assassins of Caesar. In the aftermath of the 'Ides of March' he became a fierce opponent of Mark Antony. When Antony joined Octavian and Lepidus to form the 'Second Triumvirate' in late 43 BC, Cicero was placed on a list of their enemies, captured and murdered. A significant proportion of Cicero's legal, political and philosophical writings survives. Cicero's letters, particularly those addressed to his friend Titus Pomponius Atticus, provide a wealth of detail about the events that led to the end of the Roman Republic.

The Greek historian **Lucius Cassius Dio** (*c.*AD 165–235), also known as Dio Cassius, was born in Bithynia in Asia Minor. After a successful political career in which he held the governorships of several provinces and served as consul twice, Dio wrote a history of the Roman Empire in Greek, from the legendary founding of the city up to AD 229, in 80 books. Only books 36–60 survive, which cover the period of the end of the Republic from 68 BC until AD 47. Books 41–45 cover the years 49–43 BC and describe the events of Caesar's civil war.

The poet **Lucan** (Marcus Annaeus Lucanus; AD 39–65) was a member of a powerful family from Corduba. When he was an infant, his family moved to Rome. Lucan became a close friend of the emperor Nero (r. AD 54–68), under whose patronage he achieved considerable literary success; but in AD 65, after a serious quarrel, Lucan joined in a plot to depose Nero. When his involvement was exposed, rather than face execution, Lucan chose to take his own life. He was only 25. Lucan's only surviving work is the *Pharsalia*, an epic poem about Caesar's civil war.

It begins with Caesar's crossing of the Rubicon in January 49 BC and breaks off shortly after Pompey's murder in Egypt in 48 BC. Whether the poem is incomplete because the final section has been lost, or because Lucan was still writing it when he died, is unknown.

Plutarch (c.AD 46–c.AD 120) was a philosopher and historian from Boeotia in Greece, who served as *procurator* of Achaea and a priest at Delphi. Plutarch produced works on a range of literary and scientific subjects, but the biographies of important Greek and Roman figures that make up his *Vitae Parallelae* (Parallel Lives) are his most influential. Eleven of the *Lives* concern men who featured prominently in the events that led up to the end of the Roman Republic, including Caesar, Pompey, Cicero, Crassus and Antony, and provide a great deal of detail about the period. Plutarch was deeply interested in the character of his subjects. It was probably this focus on what would now be described as 'psychology' that so attracted Shakespeare, who used the *Lives* as the source for his Roman plays, including *Julius Caesar*.

Gaius Sallustius Crispus (c.86–35 BC), known as **Sallust**, was a Roman historian who served in the army of Julius Caesar during the civil war. He had entered politics in Rome as a tribune of the plebs in 52 BC, but was later expelled from the senate. After the battle of Thapsus in 46 BC, Sallust was granted the governorship of a new province, Africa Nova, which incorporated some of Juba I's old territory. Sallust exploited the province for his own gain and became enormously wealthy. He developed a lavish house and gardens in Rome, which later became a temporary residence for the emperors. After Caesar's assassination in 44 BC, Sallust concentrated on writing. His most famous works, on the war against the Numidian usurper Jugurtha (c.160–104 BC), and the conspiracy of Cataline, have survived intact.

Suetonius (Gaius Suetonius Tranquillus; c.AD 69–c.AD 122) was the author of *De vita Caesarum* (About the Life of the Caesars), a set of biographies of Julius Caesar and the first 11 emperors. He was born either in northern Africa or Rome, and his father fought in the Roman civil war that followed the death of Nero in AD 68. Suetonius was an important Roman official and used his position to access the imperial archives to research his biographies, in which much historical information is preserved. *De vita Caesarum* is also full of salacious details about the personal lives of the emperors. Suetonius' life of Julius Caesar contains several passages about the civil war, including a dramatic account of Caesar's crossing of the Rubicon.

Valerius Maximus (fl. AD 14–37) was a Roman writer active during the reign of the emperor Tiberius (r. AD 14–37). Very little is known about him. His *Factorum et dictorum memorabilium libri IX* (Nine Books of Memorable Deeds and Sayings) has survived because it was a very popular schoolbook in the Middle Ages and Renaissance, and many copies were made. It includes a confused but colourful account of the bravery of the centurion Scaeva at Dyrrachium.

Ancient works

Appian, trans. J. Carter (1996). *The Civil Wars*. London: Penguin.

Cassius Dio, trans. E. Cary (1916). *Roman History Vol. IV (Books 41–45)*. Cambridge, MA: Harvard University Press.

Cicero, trans. E.S. Shuckburgh (1908–09). *The Letters of Cicero; the whole extant correspondence in chronological order, in four volumes*. London: George Bell & Sons. Available at https://www.perseus.tufts.edu/hopper/text?doc=Perseus%3atext%3a1999.02.0022 (accessed 4 November 2024).

Julius Caesar (pseud.), trans. A.G. Way (1955). *Alexandrian War, African War, Spanish War*. Cambridge, MA: Harvard University Press.

Julius Caesar, trans. J.F. Gardner (1967). *The Civil War together with The Alexandrian War, The African War and The Spanish War by other Hands*. London: Penguin.

Julius Caesar, trans. C. Hammond (1996). *The Gallic War*. Oxford: Oxford University Press.

Lucan, trans. S. Braund (1992). *Civil War*. Oxford: Oxford University Press.

Plutarch, trans. R. Warner (1972). *Fall of the Roman Republic*. London: Penguin.

Sallust, trans. A.J. Woodman (2007). *Cataline's War, The Jugurthine War, Histories*. London: Penguin.

Suetonius, trans. C. Edwards (2000). *Lives of the Caesars*. Oxford: Oxford University Press.

Valerius Maximus, trans. S. Speed (1678). *Memorable Deeds and Sayings*. Available at https://attalus.org/info/valerius.html (accessed 4 November 2024).

Modern works

Abdy, Richard (2024). *Legion: Life in the Roman Army*. London: The British Museum Press.

Bishop, M.C. & Coulston, J.C.N. (2006). *Roman Military Equipment from the Punic Wars to the Fall of Rome*. Second Edition. Oxford: Oxbow.

Broughton, T.R.S. (1951–86). *The Magistrates of the Roman Republic*. Three volumes. New York, NY, & Atlanta, GA: American Philological Association.

Cowan, R. (2007). *Roman Battle Tactics 109 BC–AD 313*. Elite 155. Oxford: Osprey Publishing.

Curchin, Leonard A. (1991). *Roman Spain: Conquest and Assimilation*. London: BCA.

D'Amato, R. (2011). *Roman Centurions 753–31 BC*. Men-at-Arms 470. Oxford: Osprey Publishing.

D'Amato, Raffaele & Gilbert, François (2021). *Armies of Julius Caesar 58–44 BC*. Elite 241. Oxford: Osprey Publishing.

Dobson, M. (2008). *The Army of the Roman Republic. The Second Century BC, Polybius and the Camps at Numantia, Spain*. Oxford: Oxbow Books.

Erdkamp, Paul (2010). 'Army and Society', in Nathan Rosenstein & Robert Morstein-Marx, eds, *A Companion to the Roman Republic*. Oxford: Wiley-Blackwell: pp. 278–96.

Fear, A.T. (1991). 'The Vernacular Legion of Hispania Ulterior', *Latomus*, T. 50, Fasc. 4 (OCTOBRE–DÉCEMBRE 1991): 809–21.

Feugère, Michael, trans. D.G. Smith (2010). *Weapons of the Romans*. Stroud: The History Press.

Goldsworthy, Adrian (2023). *Caesar's Civil War 49–44 BC*. Oxford: Osprey Publishing.

Goldsworthy, Adrian (2003). *The Complete Roman Army*. London: Thames & Hudson.

Keppie, Lawrence (1984). *The Making of the Roman Army: from Republic to Empire*. London: Batsford.

Konrad, C.F. (2010). 'From the Gracchi to the First Civil War (133–70)', in Nathan Rosenstein & Robert Morstein-Marx, eds, *A Companion to the Roman Republic*. Oxford: Wiley-Blackwell: pp. 167–89.

McNab, C., ed. (2010). *The Roman Army: The Greatest War Machine* in the *Ancient World*. Oxford: Osprey Publishing.

North, John. A. (2010). 'The Constitution of the Roman Republic', in Nathan Rosenstein & Robert Morstein-Marx, eds, *A Companion to the Roman Republic*. Oxford: Wiley-Blackwell: pp. 256–77.

Pollard, Nigel & Berry, Joanne (2012). *The Complete Roman Legions*. London: Thames & Hudson.

Richardson, John S. (1996). *The Romans in Spain*. Oxford: Blackwell.

Rosenstein, Nathan & Morstein-Marx, Robert, eds (2010). *A Companion to the Roman Republic*. Oxford: Wiley-Blackwell.

Sage, Michael M. (2018). *The Army of the Roman Republic: from the Regal Period to the Army of Julius Caesar*. Barnsley: Pen & Sword.

Sage, Michael M. (2008). *The Republican Roman Army: A Sourcebook*. Oxford: Routledge.

Sheppard, Si (2006). *Pharsalus 48 BC: Caesar and Pompey – Clash of the Titans*. Campaign 174. Oxford: Osprey Publishing.

Storch, R.H. (1977). 'The author of the 'De Bello Hispaniensi': a cavalry officer?', *Acta Classica* 20: 201–04.

Syme, R. (1939). *The Roman Revolution*. Oxford: Oxford University Press.

Tatum, W. Jeffery (2010). 'The Final Crisis (69–44)', in Nathan Rosenstein & Robert Morstein-Marx, eds, *A Companion to the Roman Republic*. Oxford: Wiley-Blackwell: pp. 190–211.

INDEX

References to illustrations are shown in **bold**. References to plates are shown in bold with caption pages in brackets, e.g. **54–55**, (56).